The Best Of *The Mailbox*
Primary Edition

A collection of ideas
from the first ten years of *The Mailbox* magazine

Editor in Chief: Margaret Michel

Editorial Manager: Charlotte Perkins

Editors:
Lynn Bemer

Diane Badden

Karen Shelton

Becky Simpson

Kathy Wolf

Artists:
Teresa Davidson

Teresa Fogleman

Jennifer Tipton

Irene Maag Wareham

Contributing Artist:
Terri Anderson Lawson

The Best Of *The Mailbox*

About This Book

It's been ten busy, rewarding years since we published the first issue of *The Mailbox* magazine. To celebrate, we've compiled in this volume many of the best, teacher-tested ideas published in the primary edition of *The Mailbox* since 1979. These practical ideas were sent to us by teachers across the United States. Our staff of editors selected ideas from over 50 issues to provide you with this creative and useful volume.

With *The Mailbox,* our commitment to you has always been to provide the most valuable teacher resource on the market. We take pride in bringing to you the brightest ideas and most timely teaching units. We've included many of our regularly featured sections of the magazine plus many special units.

- **Bulletin Boards:** We hope you'll involve your students in making colorful and motivating bulletin boards. Reproducible patterns make the task even easier!
- **File Folder Ideas:** Easy-to-store learning activities make basic skills fun.
- **Rainy Day Activities:** Students will love the creative art activities for every season of the year. You'll appreciate the complete instructions and inexpensive materials.
- **Lifesavers:** Management tips will help you create a positive classroom, encourage student discipline, and organize your materials.
- **Spotlight On Centers:** Adapt the easy-to-make manipulatives and learning centers to fit the needs of your students.
- **Game Plans:** Add the terrific ideas to your grab bag of individual and group games.
- **Book Specials:** To motivate reading and literature appreciation, try the activities and reproducible worksheets based on popular children's books.
- **Pocket Pals:** These creative learning activities are ready to glue on string-tie envelopes. Instructions for programming each activity with a skill are included.
- **Special Units:** We've featured many of our most popular teaching units plus reproducible worksheets. Popcorn, dental health, money, parent conferences, and doughnuts are just some of the helpful topics.
- **Our Readers Write:** We love hearing from all of you, and one thing we often hear is that this section of teaching tips is a favorite!
- **Reproducible Patterns and Worksheets:** You'll find practical, creative reproducibles that you'll use again and again.

Table Of Contents

Welcome students into your classroom on a "beary" positive note. Duplicate the bear pattern (page 25) on construction paper. Cut out and label with each student's name, or have the students do this. Mount the cutouts on the bulletin board.

Janice Hanson
West Henrietta, NY

This bus is now boarding for a great school year. Show teachers in the drivers' seats and students in the passenger section. Get student photos from their teacher from last year or from home.

Connie Stark
Jenkintown, PA

Enlist student help to make a yearlong bulletin board. In September have students draw and cut out pictures of their faces. Post on a bulletin board and top with name crowns. Each month, change the board title and student-made hats to fit the season.

October: Draw colorful masks to cover faces; November: Add decorated headbands with name feathers; December: Top with elves' hats or reindeer antlers; January: Use toboggans and scarves; February: Make heart-shaped hats; March: Make shamrock hats; April: Add bunny ears; May: Attach cut-out sunglasses.

Mary Dinneen
Bristol, CT

Welcome a new batch of students to your classroom. Enlarge the chef pattern on page 24. Label cut-out cookies with student names or pictures. Make a three-dimensional cookie sheet by covering poster board with aluminum foil and folding up one end. For a personal touch, write your name or a welcome message on the chef's hat.

Ann Louise Melnick
Lansford, PA

Along with a cute illustration of an elephant (page 24), post a plastic bag labeled with each student's name. Each morning discuss the classroom rule for the day. At the end of the day, reward those students who obeyed the rule with a paper peanut for their bags. Ten peanuts earn a special treat!

Mary Dinneen
Bristol, CT

Turn an old pair of jeans into an eye-catching helpers board. Cut several inches from the legs of an old pair of jeans. Use the scrap material to sew on additional, labeled pockets. Place name cards in the pockets. Add a bright pair of suspenders.

Susan W. Foster
Tulsa, OK

Use this bulletin board for a quick drill on math facts. Point to a circle, then to a fish, and then to another circle. The students give the answer quickly. Change the circles to increase difficulty. A fish pattern is provided on page 21.

Sister M. Henrietta
Pittston, PA

Use this bulletin board daily to take attendance. You'll know who's present, and the children will learn their addresses quickly. As students arrive, have them tack their mice next to the correct houses. A mouse pattern is provided on page 21.

Janet Lochhead
Roanoke, VA

High atop his toadstool perch, this toad coaxes your students to read. Enlarge the toad pattern on page 26, and mount it on a bulletin board. Duplicate several copies of the fly pattern (also on page 26) to complete the display.

Tanya Wilder
Broken Arrow, OK

A catchy title and self-checking format will make this money bulletin board a favorite. Use small paper bags for pockets. Stamp coins on each and staple to the board, leaving the top open. Place a poster board answer cat in each bag. Students check their work by pulling the cat out of the bag. To vary, cut out small pictures from old workbooks and glue to the bags. The students provide the missing vowel, blend, or initial or final consonant. Patterns are provided on page 20.

Becky Simpson
Winston-Salem, NC

Have your students make colorful owls from construction paper. See the pattern on page 21. Using a 12-inch pipe cleaner for each owl, staple one end to the owl's head and the other end to the bulletin board. The movement of the air in your classroom will cause the owls to bob around as if they were flying!

Lois Greenberg
Fairlawn, NJ

Three-dimensional ghosts haunt this bulletin board. Students create ghostly scenes using colored chalk on dark paper. Then each adds a tissue ghost stuffed with cotton and tied with string at the neck.

Vivian Lynn
Piscataway, NJ

There's a big yellow moon
In the Halloween sky,
And ____ witches
Are wanting to fly.
    With only one broomstick
    To use for the night,
    They'll all share the ride.
    And, oh! What a sight!

Student-made witches and poetry are a perfect combination on this unusual, Halloween bulletin board. Copy, or have a student copy, the poem on chart paper or poster board. Mount the poem on the bulletin board. Cut out a large, yellow moon and a broom with a long stick, and staple them to the bulletin board. Enlarge and duplicate the witch on page 11 for each child. Have students color their witches and add yarn for hair. Staple the delightful witches "bumper-to-bumper" on the broomstick.

Cindy Newell
Durant, OK

To follow up a discussion of local businesses, have students design and make their own shops from construction paper. This also provides good practice with possessives.

Phyllis Schweitzer
Lexington, KY

This board has many faces. Begin in October by having your students make a large, orange chain. Mount this chain in a circle as shown. In October, add a jack-o'-lantern face and stem. In November, enlarge turkey patterns on page 22. Color and mount. Children finger paint and cut out feather shapes. In December, enlarge, color, and mount patterns on page 22 for reindeer.

Wendy Shearer
Mason City, IA

Use the witch with the bulletin board on page 10 also.

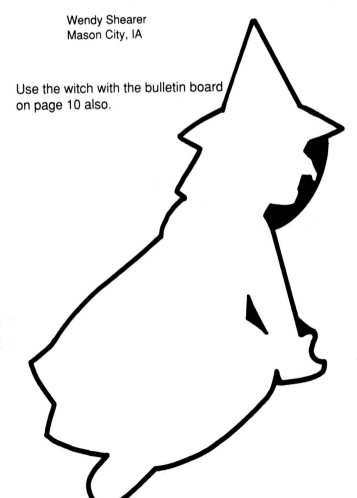

11

Hang this wreath for a holiday welcome from the kids in your class! Trace holly leaves with dark green marker, cut out, and assemble into a wreath. Tape to the door with double-sided tape. Use the pattern piece on page 19 to make beds. Insert students' school pictures snug in their beds.

Patricia A. Locke
Canal Winchester, OH

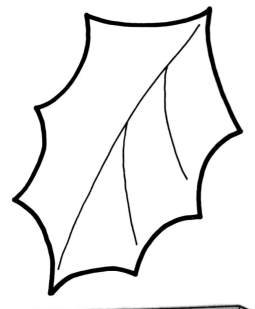

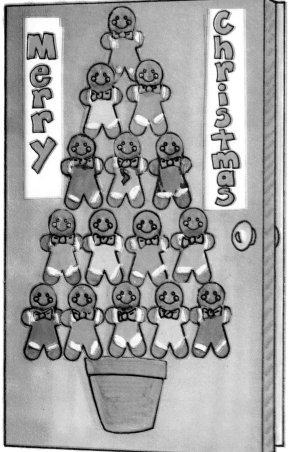

A gingerbread tree gives a holiday touch to your classroom bulletin board or door. Duplicate the gingerbread pattern (page 23) on brown construction paper for students. Each child cuts out two men and decorates one with crayons and chalk to resemble icing. Place the decorated pattern on top of the plain one. Staple the edges together as you stuff the body with old newspapers. Tie a red or green ribbon around the neck. Mount the gingerbread men in a tree shape on green background paper. Add a tree stand and title cut from red construction paper.

Lynn Morrison
Baton Rouge, LA

This door decoration is a favorite because it's edible. Tape candy canes to your door in the shape of a candy cane. Add a paper bow. On the day before Christmas vacation, let children take down the decoration and enjoy the candy!

Michelle Martin
Macon, GA

Have students trace their handprints on construction paper for these student-made bulletin boards. Arrange the hand-shaped cutouts in the shape of a Christmas tree or wreath. For a three-dimensional effect, have students curl the fingers of the cutouts around pencils.

Joan Holesko
North Tonawanda, NY

Nancy Johnson
Greensboro, NC

Bundle up for colder weather with a bunch of bears. Duplicate a teddy bear pattern (page 25) on brown construction paper, one for each student. Have children cut out their bears. After discussing winter apparel, have students "dress" their bears with winter clothing made from construction paper and fabric scraps. Mount the cutouts on winter snowbanks for a charming display.

Dianne Krieser
Waverly, NE

These bears are dressed for success in their respective careers. Duplicate a bear pattern (page 25) for each child. Ask students to choose careers that they want to pursue. Have each child cut paper or fabric clothing to dress his bear for the job.

Dianne Krieser

A bouquet of personalized hearts tells your students they are special on Valentine's Day and throughout the year. Staple paper hearts attached to colored pipe cleaners to the bulletin board. Label a cut-out paper basket with a "hearty" message for your class.

Have children stuff a huge, fabric valentine for a large-hearted classroom message. Fold one yard of red and white striped material in half. On the fold, cut out half of a heart. Open and staple loosely to the board. Stuff with plastic bags or newspapers. Staple around edges, and add a gathered toilet tissue ruffle.

Dianne West
Alto, TX

For this egg hunt, you need to scramble spelling words and write them on Easter egg cutouts. Cut green paper into strips and staple on the board to hide the eggs in. Students find the eggs and write their words correctly. Use the rabbit pattern on page 19.

Lorraine Richartz
Matamoras, PA

Tape a brown, paper tree to your classroom bulletin board or in the school hall. Provide blank, egg-shaped cards. Each time a child does a good deed, he writes it on an "egg" and attaches it to a tree limb. Cut a circle out of the tree trunk and place a colorful rabbit saying, "Happy Easter!" inside. Tape the circle over the rabbit to make a flap. Children love lifting the flap to read the secret message!

Mary Ann Proffitt
Pilot Knob, MO

16

Have your students paint small paper plates with tempera. Add construction paper fins, mouths, and tails. A little foil will add to the effect. An attractive board with little effort by the teacher!

Bonnie A. Keating
North Attleboro, MA

These baseball pals pitch in for a super summer countdown. Pin up a new baseball each day to remind everyone that it won't be long before they reach home plate! Use the patterns on page 18.

Bulletin Board Patterns

Use these patterns with "Strike The Days Till School's Out!" on page 17.

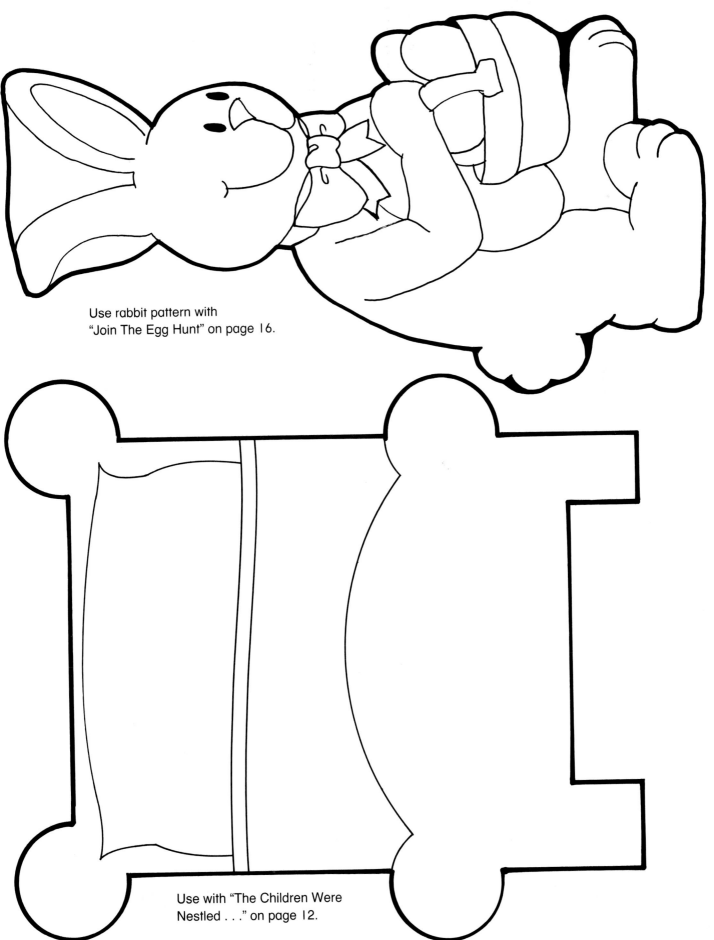

Use rabbit pattern with
"Join The Egg Hunt" on page 16.

Use with "The Children Were
Nestled . . ." on page 12.

Bulletin Board Patterns

Use with "The Cat's Out Of The Bag" on page 8.

Use with "Who's Who?" on page 9.

Use with "Little Mouse, Find Your House" on page 7.

Use with "Fishy Facts" on page 7.

Bulletin Board Patterns

Use with the bulletin boards
on page 11.

Bulletin Board Pattern

Use with "Merry Christmas" on page 12.

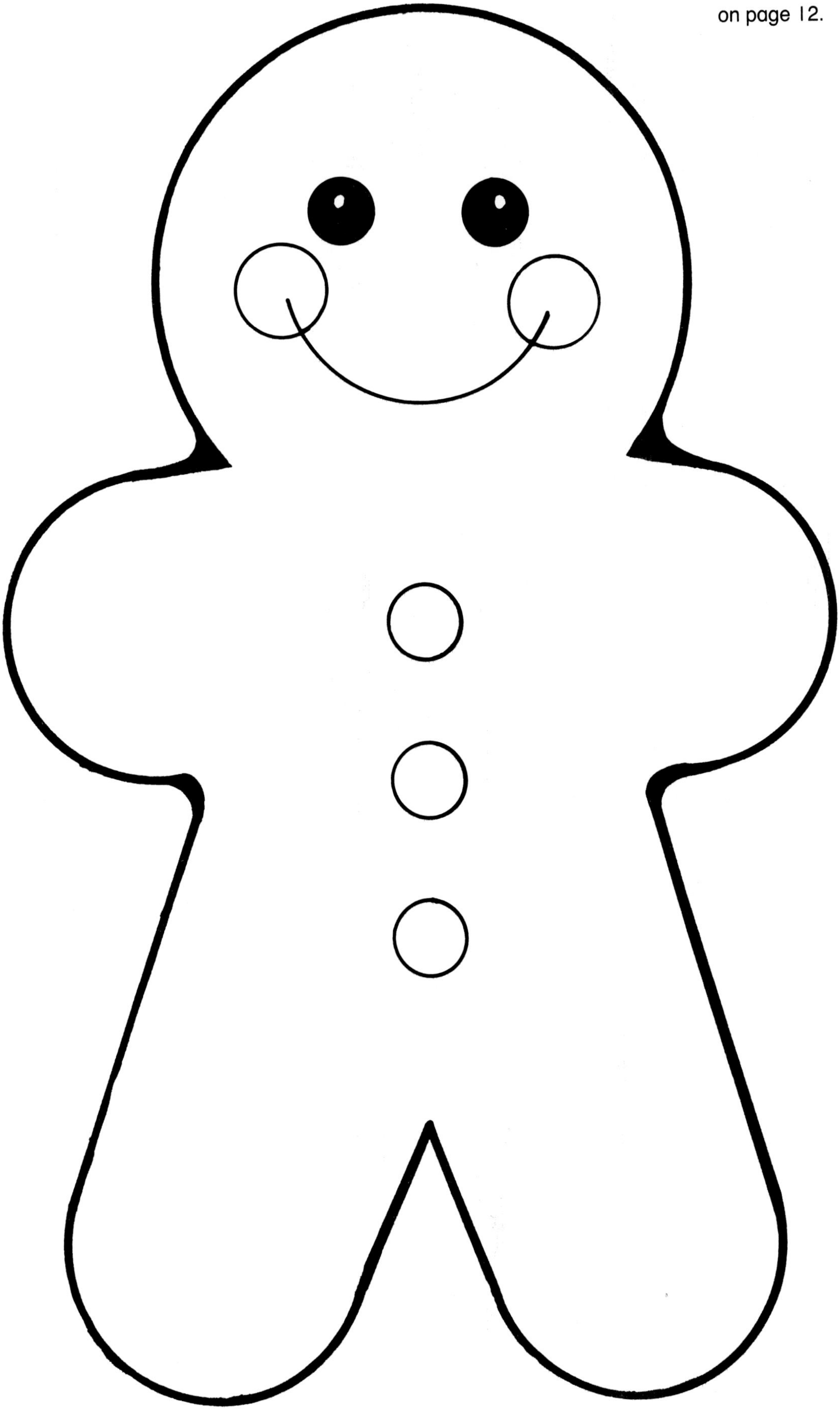

Bulletin Board Patterns

Use elephant with "Elephants Don't Forget—How About You?" on page 6.

Use chef with "A New Batch Of Students" on page 5.

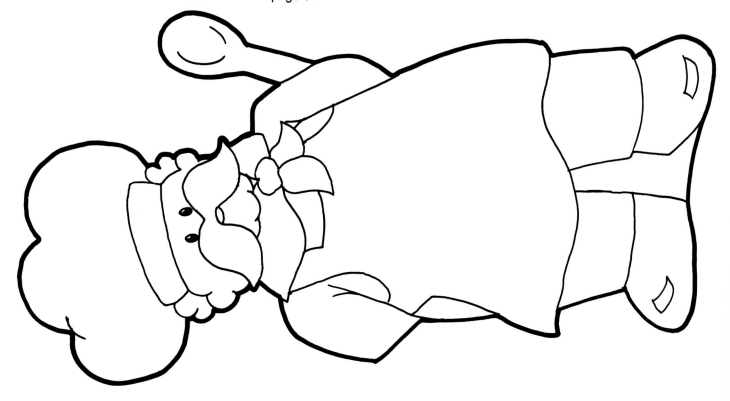

Use bear with
"Have A Beary Good
Year!" on page 4
and both bulletin
boards on page 14.

Bulletin Board Patterns

Use with "When In Doubt, Read To Find Out" on page 8.

File Folder Ideas

Ferry-Tail Land

Review homonyms with the help of some favorite fairy-tale characters. For easy construction, duplicate the worksheet below and cut it out. Glue inside a folder as shown. Write the answer key on the back of the folder.

Hulda Tayloe
Aulander, NC

Answer Key
1. The wolf <u>blew</u> down the houses of the first <u>two</u> pigs.
2. <u>Red</u> Riding Hood stopped and picked <u>some</u> <u>flowers</u>.
3. Snow White <u>ate</u> the <u>red</u> apple.
4. <u>Fair</u> Rapunzel let down her long golden <u>hair</u>.
5. <u>Dear</u> Cinderella went to the <u>ball</u> with the help of her <u>fairy</u> godmother.
6. The <u>Prince</u> kissed Sleeping Beauty and asked if she <u>would</u> marry him.
7. The <u>witch</u> tried to fatten up Hansel and Gretel to put <u>some</u> <u>meat</u> on <u>their</u> bones.
8. The Emperor was <u>too vain</u> to admit he did <u>not see</u> his <u>new</u> clothes.

Homonyms are words that sound alike but are spelled differently and have different meanings.

Student Directions:
The homonyms in these sentences are spelled incorrectly.
Rewrite the sentences correctly on your own paper.
Check your answers using the key on the back of the folder.

1. The wolf blue down the houses of the first too pigs.

2. Read Riding Hood stopped and picked sum flours.

3. Snow White eight the read apple.

4. Fare Rapunzel let down her long golden hare.

5. Deer Cinderella went to the bawl with the help of her ferry godmother.

6. The Prints kissed Sleeping Beauty and asked if she wood marry him.

7. The which tried to fatten up Hansel and Gretel to put sum meet on there bones.

8. The Emperor was two vane to admit he did knot sea his knew clothes.

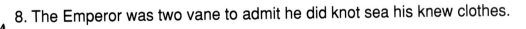

File Folder Ideas

Folder Ghosts

Ghosts of social studies definitions haunt this file folder. Matching, see-through ghosts have vocabulary words on them. Place three layers of clear Con-Tact paper or laminating film together. Cut out ghosts, and label words with permanent marker so children can see the definitions shining through. Make ghosts self-checking by matching spooky eyes.

Susan Reinagel
Benton, MO

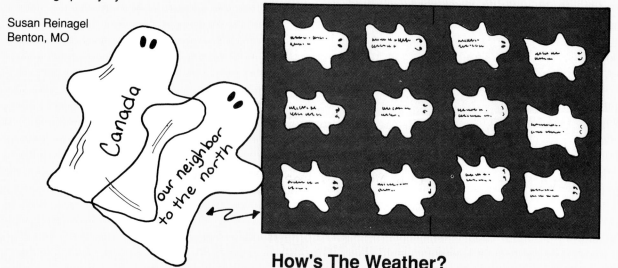

How's The Weather?

Make these pockets for sorting activity-temperature cards using the Celsius scale. For self-checking, code the back of each card. Students also enjoy converting the cards to Fahrenheit temperatures.

Fran Petersen
North Tonawanda, NY

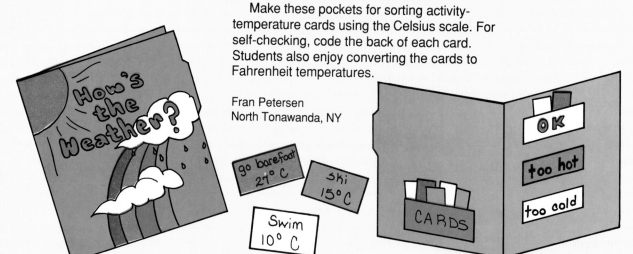

Underwater Adventure

Here is a two-person file folder activity which also works well with diphthongs or blends. To add spice, make some wild cards without a match.

Student Directions:

1. Sit on opposite ends of the board (labeled A & B).
2. Take turns picking the top card from the pile.
3. Identify the picture. Place it on an appropriate air bubble.
4. First person to cover all bubbles wins.

Marjorie Linhares
Portsmouth, RI

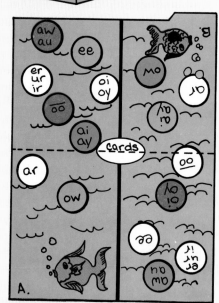

A Pocketful Of Pronouns

Label paper buttons with pronouns for this matching activity. Staple a cloth pocket inside a file folder to hold buttons. Have students cover circled words with the pronoun button needed in each sentence. Provide an answer key on the back of the folder or in the pocket.

Lois D. Duncan
Whigham, GA

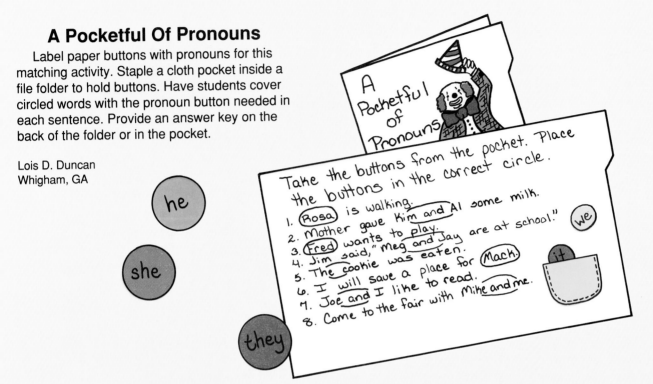

Christmas Vocabulary

Use colorful holiday stickers or gift tags to make this vocabulary activity. Children place word cards beside the matching pictures. Code the backs of the cards for easy self-checking.

Doris Perry
East Springfield, PA

File Folder Ideas

Time To Learn

Use a brad to make the hands of this front cover clock movable.

Arnetra Terry
Manson, NC

ABC Snowmen

In a file folder, draw three snowmen and attach paper clips down the front of each. On each snowman's hat, write a pair of guide words. Children clip word "buttons" in alphabetical order on the appropriate guide word snowman. To make the activity self-checking, slip answer keys into pockets on the snowmen's hats.

Glenna Sternin
North Tonawanda, NY

A Mouthful Of Math

For easy adaptability, laminate this folder, program problems with a permanent marker, and change problems when needed.

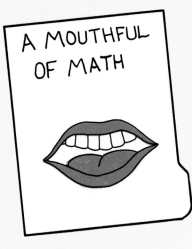

Broken Hearts

Patch up these brokenhearted fact families. Label heart cutouts with facts. Cut apart and place into a pocket attached to the folder. Students "mend the hearts" by placing each piece on the correct answer. Code the backs of the pieces for self-checking.

Laura Bartlett
Normal, IL

Mend these hearts! Place each piece on the correct heart.

Place these on this.

Big Burger Attack

Build a variety of activities around one popular theme. Label cut-out hamburgers with math problems and store in a box for Activity 6. Provide a cookbook.

Ann Bonk
Appleton, MN

File Folder Ideas

Endless Expressions

Draw two blank faces, one male and one female, on the inside of a file folder. Provide facial cutouts for students to make endless arrangements. This serves as a good story or discussion starter.

Mary Kay Carroll
Carol Doer
Sheridan, WY

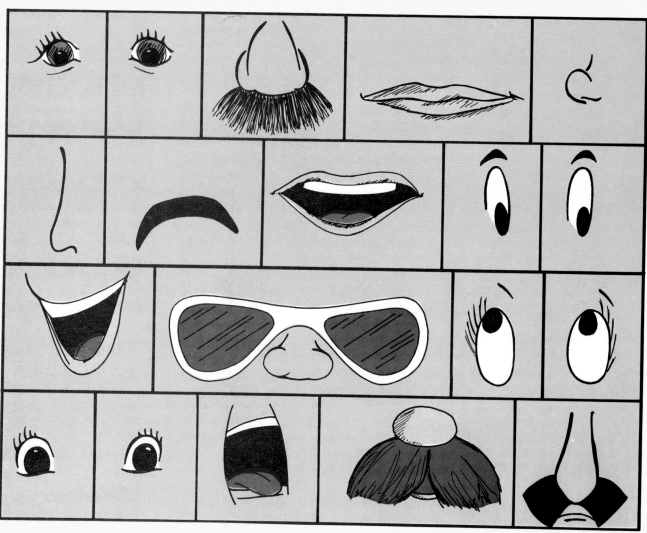

RAINY DAY ACTIVITIES

Safety Matches

Highlight Fire Prevention Week with large safety matchbooks. Cut out construction paper matches using the pattern. Glue a red cut-out circle to each tip. Label each match with a fire safety rule. To make the book, fold up 3/4" at the bottom of a 6" x 12" piece of construction paper. Glue matches in fold and staple flap to hold. Fold the matchbook cover down and label with the student's name.

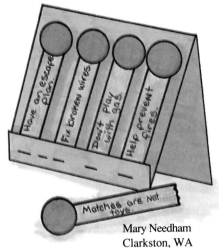

Mary Needham
Clarkston, WA

Pattern for Matches

Sample Rules:
Matches are not toys.
Have an escape plan.
Fix broken wires.
Don't play with gas.
Help prevent fires.

Friendship Rainbow

Join hands to make a friendship rainbow! Cooperation creates a cheerful bulletin board or wall decoration. Give each child a piece of 8 1/2" x 11" white paper and a specific color to paint. Children work in pairs. One child paints the partner's hands and helps to press painted hands onto the paper. When both children have made handprints and the paint is dry, the prints are cut out and mounted with others in the form of a rainbow.

Sr. Margaret Ann
Emmitsburg, MD

Crayon Batik

Batik is a textile craft that lends itself to interesting effects with crayons. To experiment with this art method in your classroom, use bright crayons to draw and color a design on a piece of white paper. Place the drawing in a pan of water. Remove after a couple of minutes. Gently ball up the picture to crinkle the paper. Flatten out the drawing on dry newspaper. Paint one shade of watercolor over the entire drawing. Quickly dip it back into the water. Remove and allow to dry flattened out on newspaper.

Betsy Kilmer
Martinsburg, WV

RAINY DAY ACTIVITIES

Jack-O'-Lanterns

Follow these directions for jack-o'-lantern faces that peek from inside orange pumpkins.

1. Cut a rectangle and eight strips of paper twice as long as the width of the rectangle.
2. Decorate the rectangle with a jack-o'-lantern face.
3. Glue side edges to form a cylinder.
4. Glue ends of each strip inside the cylinder at top and bottom edges.
5. Add green or brown paper stem.

Margie Kirk
Antigo, WI

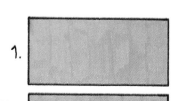

Egg Carton Witches

With a little yarn and paper, your children can change an egg carton into a real wicked witch.

1. Cut the bottom half of one egg carton so you have three sections. The divisions in the center of this piece will serve as the nose and the chin.
2. Cut black hat, eyes, and mouth from construction paper and glue on.
3. Cut strands of black yarn about 16" long and glue to the top of the "head."

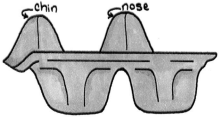

Marshmallow Spook Tree

Count down the days until Halloween with your own class Spook Tree. Cover 31 marshmallows with Kleenex, and tie with string or yarn. Add facial features with a marker and hang on a tree branch. Then have a different child remove a spook each day during October.

Karen Adams Stone
Goodland, KS

Spookies

What are scary to look at and easy to make and taste like cookies? To find out, supply the kids with these ingredients and let them invent their own Halloween treats:

plain cookies   a jar of marshmallow creme   chocolate chips
candy corn   peanuts   raisins
Reese's Pieces

After spreading a thin layer of marshmallow creme on cookies, children can make ghoulish faces by sticking on any of these items.

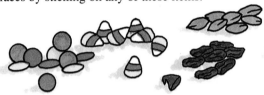

Circle Bats

Every student will want to make one of these scary creatures! Begin with two black construction paper circles. Cut one in half with a zigzag and you've got wings! Paste wings to the remaining circle; then cut a small slit in the body. Attach yarn and hang from the ceiling.

Virginia Martin
Blacksburg, VA

Rice Paper

This delicate paper provides a lovely background or decoration with a natural theme.

You will need (for each student):
Dried flowers, leaves, small plants (pressed and dried under heavy books for several weeks)
One 8" x 11" sheet of white wrapping tissue paper
One sheet of construction paper laminated or covered with Saran Wrap
White glue and water mixed to a milky consistency
Large watercolor brush
Cup for glue mixture

Fold the tissue paper in half and lay it on the construction paper. Open tissue paper flat, and arrange the pressed flowers and plants on the bottom half. Fold the top half over and smooth it. Lightly coat the entire sheet of folded paper with the glue mixture, using the brush. Wet the paper thoroughly to the edges, but don't brush over it so much that the paper tears.

Let the paper dry four to five hours, not touching it until completely dry. When dry, gently peel tissue from the construction paper and trim edges evenly. Use "rice" paper to make pages for haiku booklets or miniature folding screens and window decorations. To use it for stationery, write with ballpoint pen.

Jan Hodgin
High Point, NC

RAINY DAY ACTIVITIES

1. ↖Fold
2.
3. Glue Here
4. ↖Cut
5.
6,7

Folded-Paper Turkey

Stuff these paper turkeys for Thanksgiving party favors.

Materials: scissors, crayons, stapler, glue, and construction paper—a 12" x 12" brown piece for the body, a 2 1/2" x 7" red piece for the head, a small yellow piece, and six colored pieces for the feathers

Directions:
1. Fold the 12" x 12" piece of paper as shown.
2. Cut on the center fold line halfway up.
3. Refold into kite shape. Fold right leg. Fold left leg. Staple right leg over left leg.
4. Cut out a red turkey's head.
5. Cut a triangular beak from yellow construction paper. Paste the beak on the head. Add an eye and slip head onto body.
6. Cut and paste feathers onto body.
7. Fill turkey with popcorn, peanuts, or raisins.

Sharon Conley
Keansburg, NJ

Paper Plate Turkey

Students will enjoy making this colorful hanging turkey. Each child will need a white paper plate, two 6" circles of brown construction paper, a round toothpick, yellow and red construction paper, sixteen 4" circles of construction paper, a 4" x 2" piece of brown construction paper, glue, corn, and scissors.

Directions:
1. Cut out a section of the rim of the paper plate as shown.
2. Cut out turkey's feet.
3. Glue the feet to the back of the paper plate so they hang down in the cut-out section.
4. Glue a 6" brown circle over the feet to cover the back of the plate.
5. To make a cone shape for the turkey's body, cut the other brown circle from the edge to the center; then make 1/2" cuts at intervals around the circle. Glue the edges of the circle together, as shown. Glue cone to plate.
6. Cut wattle from red paper.
7. Fold brown rectangle and cut as shown.
8. Glue as shown with the toothpick inside the fold.
9. To make eyes, glue pieces of corn to the head.
10. For the feathers, cut out the 16 circles. Fold them in half and cut a 1" slit in the center. Slide circles onto plate.
11. To attach the head, insert toothpick in cone. Hang turkeys from the ceiling.

Ruth Thomann
Noble, IL

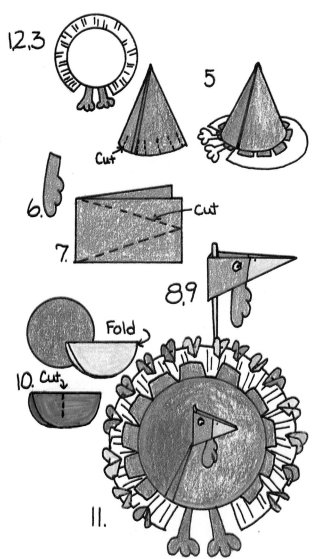

1,2,3
5
Cut
6.
7.
8,9
Fold
10. Cut
11.

Fishbowl Fun

Trace a fishbowl on a folded piece of waxed paper and cut out the two bowls. Cut goldfish, plant shapes, etc., from construction paper, adding details with crayons. Arrange the fish and plants on one of the bowls. Add crayon chips to the bottom of the bowl. Place the other bowl on top and press with a warm iron until sealed. Display the bowls in the windows or hang from the ceiling.

Janice Lester
Memphis, TN

RAINY DAY ACTIVITIES

Turkey Stuffing

Place crumpled newspaper in a brown grocery bag. Twist the top of the bag into a turkey neck and head, about half the length of the bag. Use felt or construction paper for the wattle, beak, eyes, wings, tail feathers, and feet. This is one turkey that's in the bag!

Barbara Meyers
Denville, NJ

Dreidel, Dreidel

Use your students' leftover milk cartons to make dreidels. Cover the sides of each carton with paper, and program with math problems, sight words, or review questions. Open the carton top, place a pencil in the middle, and staple back together, making sure the pencil is secure. Tape the pencil to the carton so that the pencil will not move. Students can decorate the carton with markers, chalk, glitter, cutouts, etc.

Tree Decoration

Ask parents to save scoops from coffee and powdered drink mixes. Cover the scoops completely with foil. Fill with artificial greens, tiny pinecones, pearls, etc. Put ribbon around sides and tie bow. Put a loop of yarn for hanging. Fran tells us that even those made by first-graders turned out nicely. They were creative and appreciated by parents.

Fran Petersen
North Tonawanda, NY

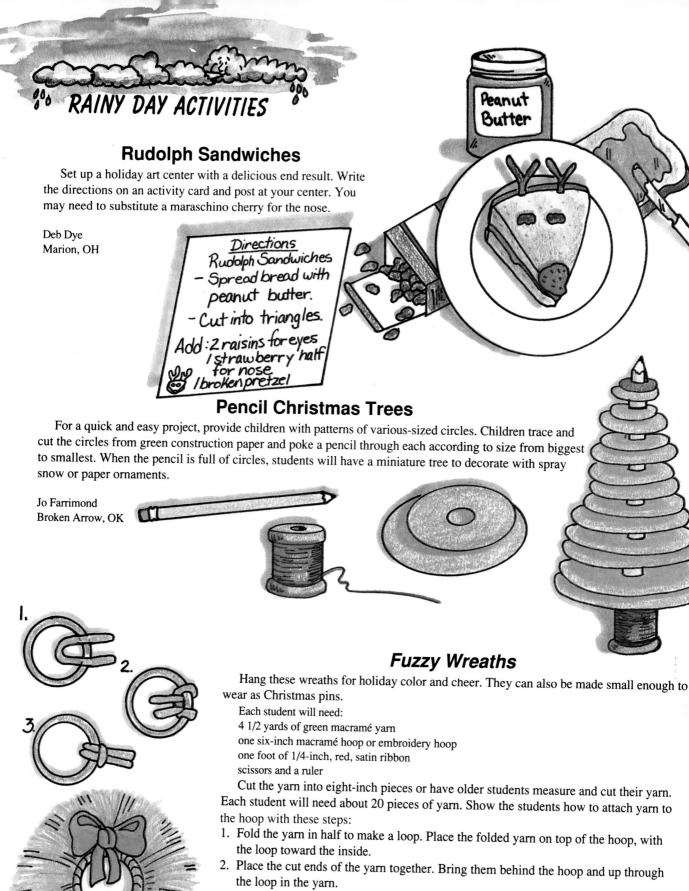

RAINY DAY ACTIVITIES

Rudolph Sandwiches

Set up a holiday art center with a delicious end result. Write the directions on an activity card and post at your center. You may need to substitute a maraschino cherry for the nose.

Deb Dye
Marion, OH

> *Directions*
> *Rudolph Sandwiches*
> *- Spread bread with peanut butter.*
> *- Cut into triangles.*
> *Add: 2 raisins for eyes*
> *1 strawberry half for nose*
> *1 broken pretzel*

Pencil Christmas Trees

For a quick and easy project, provide children with patterns of various-sized circles. Children trace and cut the circles from green construction paper and poke a pencil through each according to size from biggest to smallest. When the pencil is full of circles, students will have a miniature tree to decorate with spray snow or paper ornaments.

Jo Farrimond
Broken Arrow, OK

Fuzzy Wreaths

Hang these wreaths for holiday color and cheer. They can also be made small enough to wear as Christmas pins.

Each student will need:
4 1/2 yards of green macramé yarn
one six-inch macramé hoop or embroidery hoop
one foot of 1/4-inch, red, satin ribbon
scissors and a ruler

Cut the yarn into eight-inch pieces or have older students measure and cut their yarn. Each student will need about 20 pieces of yarn. Show the students how to attach yarn to the hoop with these steps:

1. Fold the yarn in half to make a loop. Place the folded yarn on top of the hoop, with the loop toward the inside.
2. Place the cut ends of the yarn together. Bring them behind the hoop and up through the loop in the yarn.
3. Pull both ends of the yarn to tighten the knot. Children continue to loop and knot each piece of yarn in this manner, side by side, all the way around the hoop. When hoop is full, fray the macramé yarn to make a fluffy wreath. Add a ribbon bow.

Laurie Vent
Upper Sandusky, OH

38

Christmas Cards

These greeting cards are both eye-catching and simple to make! Fold any size of red or green construction paper in half. Stick on white loose-leaf reinforcements in a simple holiday shape. Add any additional cutouts—a red bow for the wreath, a star for the tree. Students write their own Christmas greetings inside.

Joan Holesko
North Tonawanda, NY

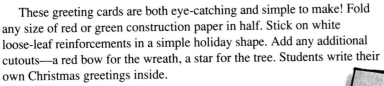

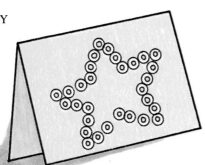

Christmas Crafts

Let the most famous reindeer of all turn your Christmas writing lesson into a special treat! Fold an 18"x4 1/2" piece of brown construction paper in half width-wise, and cut to a point at one end to form the nose. Glue two antlers and two ears behind the head. Add nose and eyes, using gummed dots for the eyeballs. Attach a piece of writing paper inside. Compose your own poem or use the one shown as your writing lesson.

Carol Wilson
Russell. KY

Christmas is coming And Rudolph is here To wish you real joy And holiday cheer!

Folded Paper Wreath

Fold a long sheet of green construction paper in half lengthwise. Fold in half again and then open the second fold. Cut slits from the folded end up to the creased line. Tape together as shown to form a circular wreath. Add a bright bow.

Nell Gardner
Warrentown, NC

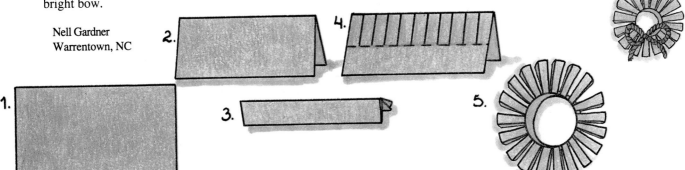

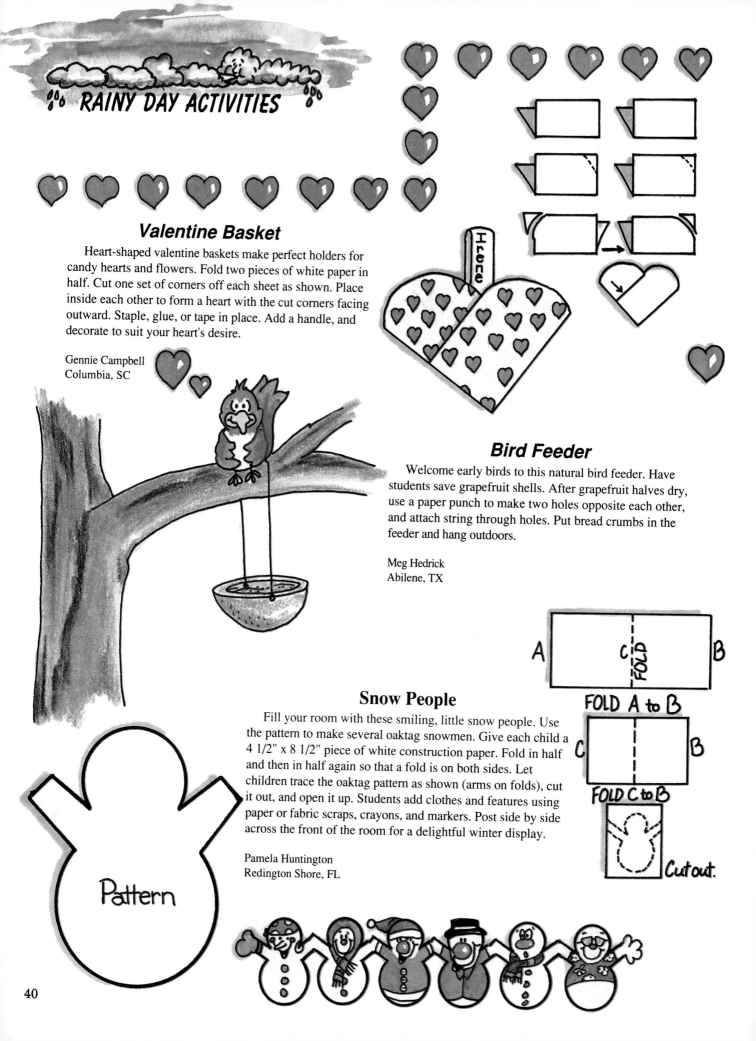

RAINY DAY ACTIVITIES

Valentine Basket

Heart-shaped valentine baskets make perfect holders for candy hearts and flowers. Fold two pieces of white paper in half. Cut one set of corners off each sheet as shown. Place inside each other to form a heart with the cut corners facing outward. Staple, glue, or tape in place. Add a handle, and decorate to suit your heart's desire.

Gennie Campbell
Columbia, SC

Bird Feeder

Welcome early birds to this natural bird feeder. Have students save grapefruit shells. After grapefruit halves dry, use a paper punch to make two holes opposite each other, and attach string through holes. Put bread crumbs in the feeder and hang outdoors.

Meg Hedrick
Abilene, TX

Snow People

Fill your room with these smiling, little snow people. Use the pattern to make several oaktag snowmen. Give each child a 4 1/2" x 8 1/2" piece of white construction paper. Fold in half and then in half again so that a fold is on both sides. Let children trace the oaktag pattern as shown (arms on folds), cut it out, and open it up. Students add clothes and features using paper or fabric scraps, crayons, and markers. Post side by side across the front of the room for a delightful winter display.

Pamela Huntington
Redington Shore, FL

A c FOLD B

FOLD A to B

C B

FOLD C to B

Cutout.

Pattern

40

Valentine Award

Even young students can make attractive valentine award corsages using just construction paper and glue. Each child will need nine 5" x 3/4" strips of construction paper. To make, glue one end of each strip to the back of a small cut-out heart. After drying, fold each strip in, towards the center, and glue to the back to make a loop. Attach small hearts to the ends of several more strips and glue to the back for streamers. Students use markers or glitter to decorate the hearts. Use the corsages as student awards or parent valentines.

Debbie Wiggins
Myrtle Beach, SC

Valentine Mouse

Trap students' interest with these valentine mice treats. For each mouse, cut a five-inch red square of construction paper or felt into a heart. Glue top edge as shown. Cut and glue on two heart ears. Add wiggly eyes; then color a nose and whiskers. Insert a valentine pencil from The Education Center or a lollipop so that the end sticks out for a tail. Add a message on mouse if desired.

Annette Mathias
Partridge, KS

Woven Hearts

Use small strips of paper and heart outlines to weave unique valentines. Children fold construction paper hearts in half and cut slits. They open and weave with contrasting color strips. A valentine message written on top and cut-out hearts at the ends of the strips will make these special gifts for special people.

Mary Ann Kiessling
Oaklyn, NJ

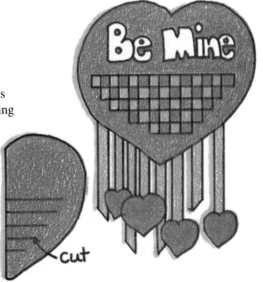

Potato Monsters

When you create these wrinkled monsters, they continue to grow strange appendages. To make a monster, each child will need a sprouting potato, a metal jar lid, a nail, scraps of tissue paper, glue, a pair of wiggly eyes, and watercolor paints. Without breaking off sprouts, children paint their potatoes and sprouts in contrasting colors. Next, each child drives a nail through his jar lid and covers the lid with tissue paper. After mounting painted potatoes on nails, students glue on eyes and other materials to create "spuds from space" or Irish gnomes.

Betty Brooks
Filer, ID

nail

Jar Lid

Easter Bunny

Hatch a cotton ball Easter bunny! Make the upper part of a rabbit by gluing cotton balls to construction paper. Then decorate a paper egg and cut along a zigzag line. Glue in place, slipping the upper half under the bunny and the bottom half over him.

Barbara Baum
Navaire, OH

Look What Hatched!

Combine art and creative writing for a fun and fanciful language arts activity. Each child writes a story about finding a rather unusual Easter egg—instead of hatching a chick, it hatched some other animal! After finishing the story, students cut a large wallpaper egg in half and then hinge the halves with a brad so that they open and close. Glue a cutout of the animal inside the egg and post it, with the story, on a bulletin board.

Betty Bowlin
Chesterfield, MO

Rainbow For Springtime

Colorful hanging rainbows fight off the winter gloom in your classroom. Provide each student with four brightly colored pipe cleaners with chenille stems, glue, cotton, and plastic fishing line. Have students form each pipe cleaner into a circle shape and then allow it to spring back to form an arc. Glue the four curved pipe cleaners together to form a rainbow. Add a puffy cotton cloud at each end. Suspend from the lights or ceiling with fishing line.

C. Stark
Chittenham, PA

Fresh Spring Hyacinths

Your classroom will bloom with these spring flowers. Each child needs a toilet paper tube, scissors, glue, 1 1/2" squares of purple and pink tissue paper, a pencil, a plastic straw, floral tape, and green construction paper. Staple one end of the tube and cut it to a rounded shape. Have children cover the tube with the tissue by folding each square, one at a time, over the end of a pencil. Dab each piece lightly in glue and attach to the tube. Wind floral tape around a plastic straw and attach as a stem. Add construction paper leaves. "Plant" these pretty flowers in paper cups or post on a bulletin board.

Martha Cranfill
Chicago, IL

Spring Lambs

Welcome spring with a flock of woolly lambs. Have each student trace his hand on black construction paper and cut out the shape. Each child glues a wiggly eye on the thumb and cotton balls to fill in the body. Each black sheep gets a colorful bow on his neck.

Betty Brooks
Filer, ID

43

RAINY DAY ACTIVITIES

Flowerpot Pencil Holder

Use a sand-filled flowerpot and "pencil flowers" to brighten up your room for spring. Tape or glue paper flowers to the tops of pencils and place in the pot. Students will want to return borrowed pencils to this clever holder.

Diane Vogel
Chamblee, GA

Here's a gift for Mother's Day:
I'll try my best in every way.
But when you get upset with me,
Relax and have a pot of tea!
Love,

_____

Mother's Teakettle

This kettle card whistles a merry message for Mother's Day. Make two paper kettles for each student. Have each child decorate the front of his kettle and write this message inside. Students insert tea bags between their kettles and staple them at the top.

Sharon Conley
Keansburg, NJ

Mother's Day Bouquet

A basket of job-labeled flowers will let mom choose a gift seven days of the week. Staple or glue an eight-inch construction paper square into a cone shape, and attach a 1/2" x 6" handle. Youngsters print seven jobs they would like to do for Mom on seven-inch paper stems and attach crumpled tissue paper blossoms.

Barbara Woods
Fairfax, VA

Table Captains

I keep my classroom organized by appointing a different table captain each week. Table captains are responsible for keeping the table clean, passing out work, and passing out snacks. This practice helps students develop responsibility and overcome shyness.

At the end of each week, I reward table captains for their hard work. I put several different styles of pencils from The Education Center in a paper sack and allow each captain to select one pencil. The students love the recognition and are pleased with their gift.

Pamela Myhowich
Selah, WA

Hall Passes

Use tongue depressors for handy hall passes. Tape a picture of a nurse, telephone, or library book to each stick. Write a message on each stick, such as "This student has my permission to use the phone." Put magnetic tape on the backs of the passes, and store them on your filing cabinet.

Connie Connely
Catoosa, OK

Mailbox Organizer

To keep the "goodies" in *The Mailbox* close at hand, I paste the table of contents on the front of the magazine. I also list the reproducibles found in it. That way I don't miss any of the good ideas, and I save time, too!

Sr. Margaret Ann Wooden
Martinsburg, WV

File Folder Storage

File folder centers easily slip into The Education Center's large-sized string-tie envelopes. This makes for excellent storage when separate pieces or cards are used in the centers. Label the envelopes to identify each center, and include a list of pieces.

Geraldine Fulton
Sedgewickville, MO

Question Marks

To cut down on interruptions when working with a reading or math group, I give each child a laminated index card with a question mark on it. When a child has a question, he puts the card on the top corner of his desk. Between group activities, I go around and answer each question. Often, by the time I get to their questions, they have already figured out the answers!

Jane Dickert
Bath, SC

Line-up Flag

To curb class noise and confusion at line-up time, attach a homemade flag to an old broomstick. When classes line up to come in from outside, the teacher on duty gives the "Olympic Flag" to the quietest class. That class gets to go in first. They also receive a check mark on a hall chart. The class that earns five checks first gets a reward: free video time, free reading time, or stickers. This idea is so successful, you will have trouble deciding which class carries the flag!

Mary Dinneen
Bristol, CT

Secret Satchel

Pack a real suitcase with all learning games that students can do independently. After a child completes all of his work, he receives a key that entitles him to open the satchel and choose a game to enjoy.

Hope Speranza
Edison, NJ

Alphabetizing Valentines

Before the children give out their valentines, I have them practice arranging their cards in alphabetical order. I then post an alphabetized class list on the board. Students check the cards, then sit in the listed order. Passing out the cards is then quick and easy.

Carole Donoghue
Bristol, CT

Lifesavers

Helpful Checks

Organize your lesson plans by using a check mark whenever classroom worksheets or extra materials are needed. After preparing the materials, circle the check mark in your planbook to indicate that you are ready for the lesson. It's easy, and there are no unwanted surprises in your day.

Kathy Graham
Filer, ID

Winter Weather Help

During the start of the winter season, have each child write his name on a pinch clothespin. On days when boots are worn, each child clips his boots together with his clothespin. This makes boots readily identifiable, especially when more than one student has the same color boots!

Linda Terranora
Westerly, RI

Classwork Organizer

Students do the organizing for you with this quick trick! Label several boxes for subject or skill areas you're covering. Each day, place work assignments beside the corresponding boxes. Clip a number to each box to show which assignment needs to be done first, second, and third. When a student finishes his paper, he places it in the correct box and moves on to the next number. At the end of the day, the papers are already sorted and ready for grading.

Janice M. Thames
Thomson, GA

Workbook Record-Keeping

Attach a ditto to the back cover of your students' reading workbooks. Number it to correlate with the pages in the workbook. Each time a page is completed and graded, record the score next to the page number. This gives your students a personal record and allows you to send graded work home immediately.

Marjorie S. Martin
Elyria, OH

Folders For Reading Papers

Provide a colored pocket folder for each student. Label pockets Take-Home Papers and To-Be-Done Papers. At the end of the day, students put completed work in the To-Be-Done pocket and turn folders in. I check work and place papers in the appropriate pockets. I am the only one who may put papers in the Take-Home side. When the folders are passed out, students know immediately which papers need corrections. Extra bonus: only one thing to return to each child.

Maxine Bishop
Fairfield, IL

Special Studybooks

Here's a way to increase parental involvement in skills practice. At the beginning of the school year each student needs a notebook or composition book. Whenever a new skill is taught, students glue practice papers into their studybooks. Inform parents that when students bring the studybooks home, there is a skill to practice. The children can use their studybooks during the summer to practice and reinforce skills—an added bonus.

Sue Ireland
Mont Alto, PA

Quick Notes

Are you spending too much time writing reminders and other notes? By thinking ahead a little, you can save yourself a lot of time. Begin with a copy of your letterhead stationery. Find a clever black-line illustration and attach it to your stationery. List several of your most frequently written messages and duplicate several copies. When you need to send a note, pick up a copy of your personalized stationery and circle the message you want to convey.

Barbara Coon Roberts
Fontana, CA

File Helpers

To help organize my files, I place a piece of colored construction paper in the front of my file folders. As I use the worksheets, I place the leftover ones in front of the construction paper. I never have to guess which papers have already been used.

Kathy Graham
Filer, ID

Flower Finders

At the beginning of each school year, very young students need a lot of assistance in the lunchroom. I put bouquets of paper flowers on our assigned lunch tables so that the children will know where to sit. This frees me to help the children in the lunchline with their trays and avoids a lot of confusion.

Sheila R. Chapman
Decatur, AL

Reading Motivator

To motivate children to read, cut a commercially prepared certificate or award (one per student) into six to ten strips. Number the backs of the strips for easy reassembling and place in individual envelopes labeled with student names. For each student, glue one-half piece of ditto paper to an unusual construction paper shape, label with the student's name, and mount on a bulletin board. Each time a student reads a book, glue a strip from his envelope to his shape. A student will enjoy watching his certificate near completion each time he reads a book. When the certificate is completed, add a sticker and send it home. Also a great way to motivate good behavior.

Mary Whaley
Kentland, IN

Puzzle Power

To reduce homeroom chaos, my students may work at an ongoing puzzle table as they arrive. On rainy days, we have a puzzle contest between groups of six to eight children. Each group is given a puzzle with the same number of pieces. The group which assembles their puzzle first wins a prize.

Sr. Margaret Ann
Emmitsburg, MD

Select A Sticker

Tack up a sheet of sticker rewards in a prominent, convenient spot in the classroom. During the day, as you wish to reward a student for good behavior, call out his name. The student selects his own reward from the sheet to wear proudly.

M. Corso
Bristol, CT

Wristband Parent Notes

Primary students have a difficult time remembering to deliver notes to parents. To alleviate this problem, write parent messages on strips of tagboard. Before dismissal, tape the strip around the child's wrist and decorate with a colorful sticker. Children are proud of their wristbands, and the teacher knows his messages are getting home to parents.

John Kessler
Davenport, IA

Magic Numbers

As each child enters my class for the first time, he is given a "magic number." This number is used when textbooks are issued and throughout the year on permission slips, report cards, and other papers that must be returned. A quick check of papers will tell the teacher which ones are missing. It is easy to check papers, record grades, and file tests because the papers are always in order. We even play games, line up, and move to centers using magic numbers.

Arlene Johnston
Bradenton, FL

Kernel Quieter

Get a grip on class discipline with a popcorn surprise. Put a "frowny" face on a clear quart jar and fill the jar with unpopped popcorn. Label another quart jar with a happy face. When your class behaves well, transfer a handful of the popcorn to the "happy" jar. For undesirable behavior, move some corn from the "happy" jar back to the "sad" one. When all the popcorn gets into the "happy" jar, reward your class with a well-deserved popcorn party!

Lisa Rae Anderson
Norfolk, NE

Lifesaver Behavior

Good behavior on field trips will increase when students know they're earning lifesavers. Cut circles from colored tagboard in a size large enough to slip on wrists. Reward individuals with lifesavers during the trip for appropriate behavior. Upon return, students can trade in their lifesaver bracelets for real Lifesaver candy or a small prize.

Connie Connely
Catoosa, OK

Light The Jack-O'-Lantern

Reinforce good health habits with this clever jack-o'-lantern. Using the pattern below, make the folding pumpkin from orange construction paper and cut out facial features. Fold in half and glue along the edges, leaving the top half open. Now make two circles (one yellow and one black) to slip inside. When a student is not observing good habits, display the black circle. Light up the pumpkin when everything looks good. Works well for almost any skill.

Wilma Heiser
Falls City, NE

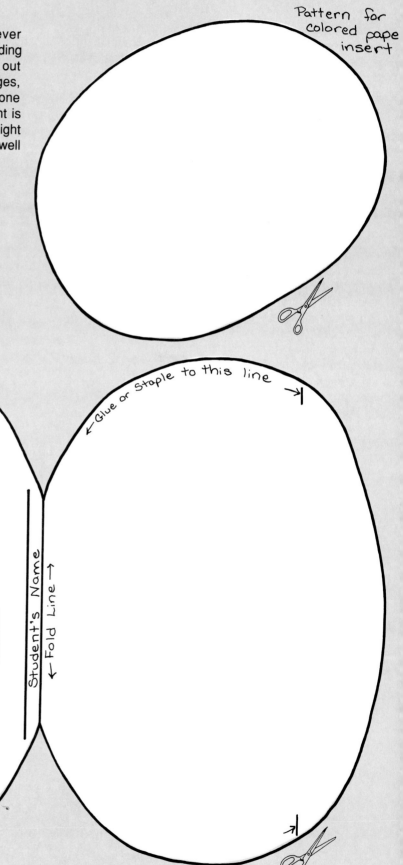

Pattern for colored paper insert

Glue or Staple to this line →

Student's Name

← Fold Line →

Cut

Cut

Cut

Cut

48

Spotlight on Centers

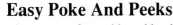

Easy Poke And Peeks

Cut out picture rows from old workbooks, and glue them to poster board. Punch a hole under each picture, and draw a ☺ on the back over the correct answer hole. Good for rhyming, visual discrimination, etc.

Elaine Belscher
Spring Hill, FL

Doughnut Boxes

Use this center idea to practice dozens of skills! Take a doughnut box apart, laminate, and staple back together. Fill with poster board doughnuts labeled with words to alphabetize, math problems, long- and short-vowel words to sort, etc.

Diane Vogel
Chamblee, GA

Chocolate Chip Count

Make a batch of laminated, chocolate chip cookie cutouts, and store in a McDonald's Chocolate Chip Cookie box. Have children count the chips and write the number on the cookie with a grease pencil.

Rhonda Rice
Catoosa, OK

Have A McNugget!

These golden nuggets of wisdom provide math practice in regrouping. Use a recycled Chicken McNuggets box to encourage children to "try a few." Each paper McNugget shape shows a regrouping math problem and a self-checking flip side. Cut shapes from yellow or brown construction paper. Program brown ones with "crunchier" problems to challenge accelerated students.

Angela Choate
Oklahoma City, OK

Magic Rabbits

Abracadabra, and students will change vowels from short to long for magical new words. Cut out hats with slots through which words on rabbits will show, and mark with a final silent *e* after the slot. On rabbit cutouts write short-vowel words that can be changed into long-vowel words by adding an *e*. Make sure that a word will be visible in the space when a rabbit is in a hat. Students match rabbits to hats to form new words.

Sandi Nolte
Lynchburg, VA

Wormy Apples

Give each child three to six apples and the same number of small worms. A "teacher" holds up or calls out a fact on a large worm. If the child has the answer, he puts a little worm through the hole in that apple. The winner is the first to have all "wormy apples."

This game is open-ended and can be used for many different content areas. Suggested variations:

—vowel sounds and words with those sounds
—topic questions and answers
—contractions and the words that make them

Nell Gardner
Warrenton, NC

True Or False

Each student has a true and a false face. See illustration. Faces can be used in a variety of ways with true and false statements. For example, a child can pick a card and hold up the correct face to answer true or false. Or the teacher can hold up a card or read a sentence, and the group responds by holding up faces. When played like "Simon Says," last child left in the game is the winner!

Jill Purdy
West Linn, OR

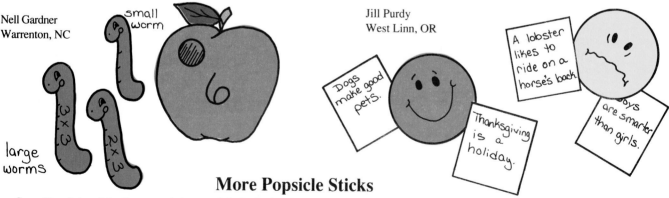

More Popsicle Sticks

Save Popsicle sticks for an activity on alphabetical order. Label sticks with words to be placed in order, and number the backs for easy self-checking. Color-code all the sticks in one set and store in a Styrofoam cup.

Karen Bellis
Stover, MO

Christmas Cookies

Use a Christmas cookie can or let students decorate a can. Provide two paper plates. Cut poster board cookies in bright colors. Write a problem on each cookie that is appropriate for your students. Number the cookies on the back and provide an answer key.

Players take turns drawing a cookie from the can and solving the problem. If player is correct he may place the cookie on his plate.

Ann Heflin
Judy Streb
Huntsville, AL

Yummy Christmas Trees

Set up a tasty learning center to sharpen direction-reading skills. Add green food coloring to canned icing and place at a center with hors d'oeuvre knives and small cookie decorations and candies. Give each child a sugar cone. Post a chart of steps for making a tree. To send home, place the finished tree inside a wide-mouthed plastic cup. Tape another cup over the top.

STEPS
1. Use a knife to cover your tree with icing.
2. Put the cone over two or three of your fingers.
3. Press candy pieces into the icing to decorate.
4. Place your tree on a paper towel to dry.
5. Clean your knife at the sink. Take it back to the center.

Sara Davis
Oklahoma City, OK

Paper Plate Centers

Party paper plates add pizzazz to any learning center with their colorful, seasonal themes and favorite children's characters. Staple a construction paper pocket to the front of the plate. Add yarn to hang. Children sort skill cards into the correct pocket and check on backs of cards for answers. To sort seasonal vocabulary words, use seasonal paper plates and matching seasonal stickers on backs of word cards for checking.

Linda Gwardiak
Georgetown, SC

ABC Wreath

Draw numbered circles on a large cut-out wreath. Write words to be alphabetized on cut-out Christmas balls. Children place the balls on the wreath in correct ABC order. Number-code the backs of the balls for easy self-checking. This holiday idea can be used with any sequential skill.

Lynne Willis
Augusta, GA

51

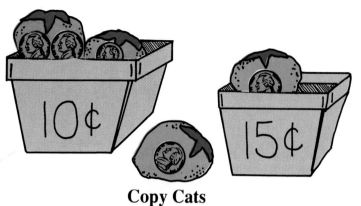

Strawberry Cents

Real berry baskets add a nice touch to a coin-reading center. Stamp coin images on strawberry cutouts and label baskets with values or money words for matching.

Ella Gainer
Mount Joy, PA

Copy Cats

Draw identical cats in two different sizes and duplicate. On the larger cat, write an uppercase word or sequence of letters. Write the same letters on the small cat in lowercase. Students match up the correct copy cats.

Lorraine Richartz
Matamoras, PA

Clever Clipsticks

Clip tongue depressors together with clothespins for a variety of matching games. Label tongue depressors with antonyms, homonyms, synonyms, contractions, possessives, or math problems and answers. Store these long-lasting wooden sets in Pringles potato chip cans.

Rhonda Thurman-Rice
Catoosa, OK

A Handful Of Math

Ask children to join hands in making a box of math task cards. Have each child trace his hand on laminated construction paper and cut out the shape. Have children write numerals on the fingers with markers. Store hands in a box with wipe-off markers. Students choose a "handful" and write the sum on each hand. Provide an answer key.

Virginia Newbold
Harrisburg, PA

Questions By The Dozen

Provide a dozen eggs for students to count coins "eggs-actly." Save an empty egg carton. Add 12 plastic eggs that come apart. Number the eggs, and put a coin or a set of coins in each. Place the eggs at a center, and provide duplicated sheets showing matching numbered eggs. Children open each egg and count the coins. They write the coin values on the corresponding eggs on the answer sheets. The eggs can also hold slips of paper with math, science, or social studies questions. Students can crack a new dozen each day!

Jan Hicks
Sewickley, PA

Window Card Workout

These window cards provide fast math practice. Write rows of addition or subtraction problems on an 8" x 11" piece of poster board. Cut a long window under each row; then turn the card over and write answers below the window so they'll correspond to the problems. Students place their papers underneath the card and write their answers in the window. To check instantly, they turn the card over and reinsert their papers. Vary with multiplication or division problems.

Mrs. Marshall Sperry
Decatur, IL

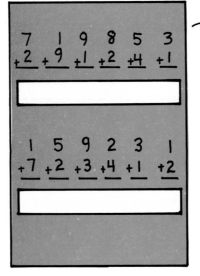

Light The Menorah

Draw a large menorah as shown and cut out a series of candles. Label one candle with a number and place it in the central position. Students write math facts equaling that number on their candles and light the menorah. This also works well for synonyms or rhyming words.

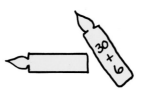

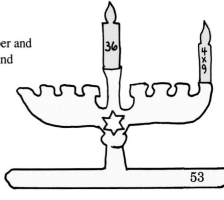

Itsy-bitsy Spider

Here's a springtime manipulative with a familiar friend. To make this spider's garden spout, cover a potato chip can with paper. Cut a slit in the plastic lid. Write sight words on a tagboard strip cut to slide through the slit. Glue a cut-out spider to the top of the strip. Students try to get the spider to the top of the "spout" by pulling the strip up as they read the words correctly. Make additional strips labeled with math facts, homonyms, or antonyms.

Diane Vogel
Chamblee, GA

Pattern

Chalkboard Strips

Take the boredom out of math drill with giant problem strips. Program poster board strips with math facts and laminate. Have a student place a strip in the chalk tray and write his answers on the board beside the strip. Program the back of the strip with answers for self-checking. Make lots of strips and hold "strip races." The first player to complete his strip correctly scores a point for his team.

Rhonda Thurman-Rice
Tulsa, OK

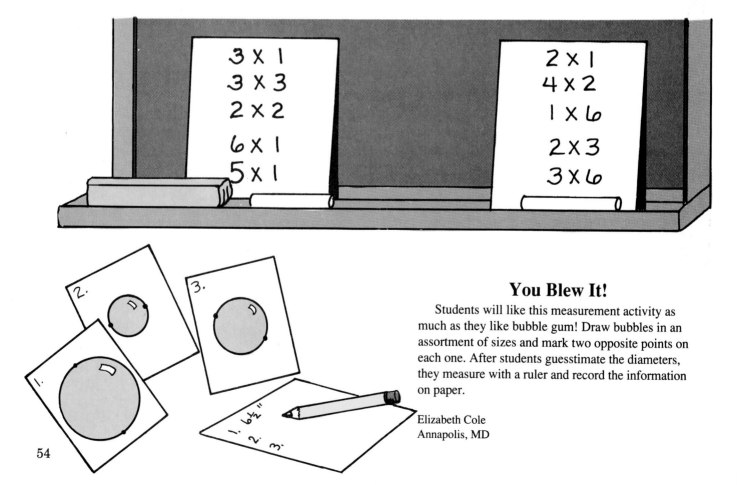

You Blew It!

Students will like this measurement activity as much as they like bubble gum! Draw bubbles in an assortment of sizes and mark two opposite points on each one. After students guesstimate the diameters, they measure with a ruler and record the information on paper.

Elizabeth Cole
Annapolis, MD

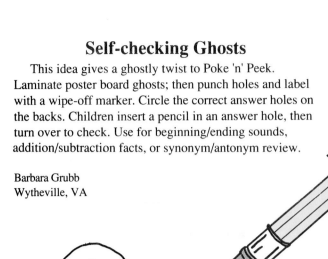

Self-checking Ghosts

This idea gives a ghostly twist to Poke 'n' Peek. Laminate poster board ghosts; then punch holes and label with a wipe-off marker. Circle the correct answer holes on the backs. Children insert a pencil in an answer hole, then turn over to check. Use for beginning/ending sounds, addition/subtraction facts, or synonym/antonym review.

Barbara Grubb
Wytheville, VA

Copy Cat Practice

For independent handwriting practice, make separate sentence strips for letters being practiced. Students select one strip and practice on the blackboard and then on handwriting paper. Silly, humorous sentences and riddles work well. Add alliteration for more fun. Put the sentence strips in a snack can decorated with Con-Tact paper and cat stickers. Here are some sample copy cat sentences:

Mary Anne Haffner
Waynesboro, PA

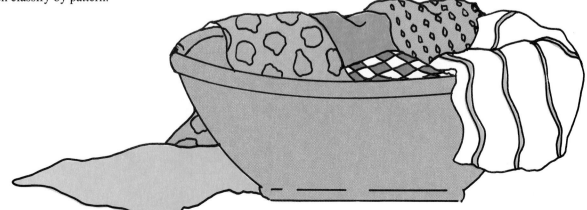

Silly Sammy

Felix Feline found friends in France.

Charlie Cougar caught cold in his Cadillac.

Copy Cat Practice

Lennie Leopard likes licorice.

Scrap Sort

Collect scraps of fabrics with different patterns—striped, plaid, plain, polka-dot, flowered, etc. Place the scraps in an old purse or sewing basket. Children classify by pattern.

Can O' Worms

Cover two empty cylinders and label each one Can O' Worms. Cut 40 pieces of brown yarn—each four inches long. Make 40 problem cards using skills you are currently working on.

Student Instructions for 2 Players: Place the cards facedown. Draw one at a time. If solved correctly, take a worm from the stack and put it in your can. Continue until all problems are solved. The player with the most worms is the winner.

Ann Heflin
Judy Streb
Huntsville, AL

Create A Story

Cover a box with gift wrap. (A box from ditto masters is perfect size.) Collect lots of pictures from magazines or workbooks. Paste each on a 3" x 5" card. Make a set of ditto sheets (see illustration). Print directions inside the box lid.

Directions: Select a picture, paste it on the ditto sheet, and write a creative story. Later share it with the class.

Fran Petersen
North Tonawanda, NY

Ketchup Or Mustard?

Students get to add ketchup or mustard to these hot dogs for noun/verb practice. Cut out hot dog shapes and laminate. Program with nouns and verbs. Provide red and yellow wipe-off crayons to mark nouns with ketchup and verbs with mustard.

Susan Child
Front Royal, VA

The Rat Brigade!

Your Rat Brigade activity board may be used for various skills by simply changing the ears in the pocket. We have shown it with proper and improper fractions. The following are possible variations: antonyms, multiplication, numbers and sets, parts of speech, colors/color words.

Arlene Novels
Indiana, PA

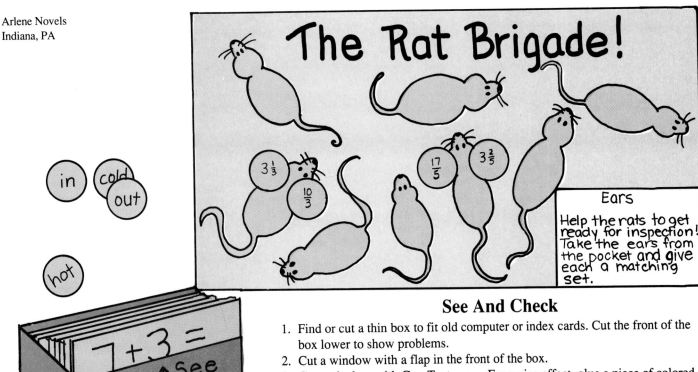

See And Check

1. Find or cut a thin box to fit old computer or index cards. Cut the front of the box lower to show problems.
2. Cut a window with a flap in the front of the box.
3. Cover the box with Con-Tact paper. For a nice effect, glue a piece of colored plastic inside the window.
4. Write a problem on each card. Write the answer so it shows in window under flap.

The pupil answers the problem and lifts flap to check answer. If correct he removes card. If not, he returns it to the back of the stack. This can be adapted to any skill or grade level.

Fran Petersen
N. Tonawanda, NY

Disappearing Ghosts

Paste, copy, or enlarge the ghost on poster board. Write a vowel combination on each piece. Cut it into puzzle pieces. Assemble.
Variations:
Sight words—The child reads the word shown.
Syllabication—The child tells the number of syllables in the word shown.
Prefixes—The child identifies prefix in the word shown.
Synonyms—The child gives a synonym for the word shown.
Student Directions:
Choose a section of the ghost. If you can give a word with that vowel combination, you may remove that part and help the ghost disappear.

Ann Price
Ridgeway, VA

Spotlight on Centers

Hanging in Place

Children get the hang of place value concepts with the help of a coat hanger. Cover the hanger with wallpaper and fold up to form a pocket. Divide into three smaller pockets, label, and use Popsicle sticks as counters. For language arts, write rhyming words on the pockets and sticks.

Elizabeth Cole
Annapolis, MD

Vegetable Patches

Try these vegetable patches for a review center on language skills.

Debbie Smith
Port Jervis, NY

The Ice Cream Center

A Styrofoam cooler makes a perfect display for a center on any subject or theme. Simply turn it upside down and use thumbtacks to mount cards, pockets, and pieces. Marianne uses her cooler as a language arts center. Here is what she displays on each of the four sides:
1. Colorful picture of ice cream and general directions.
2. A pocket containing cards with an ice-cream flavor written on each. Children alphabetize flavors.
3. Story with dittoed comprehension questions.
4. Cones with short stories and ice-cream scoops with appropriate titles to be matched to cones.

Marianne Shoemaker
Silver Springs, MD

Early Reading Puzzles

Use small paper plates or Styrofoam trays from the grocery store. Paste a picture on one half. Write the corresponding word on the other half. Cut in jigsaw puzzle shapes. Put pieces of five or six words in a set. Store the set in a plastic bag.

These puzzles are quiet and easy and give children a great sense of accomplishment early in reading.

Fran Petersen
North Tonawanda, NY

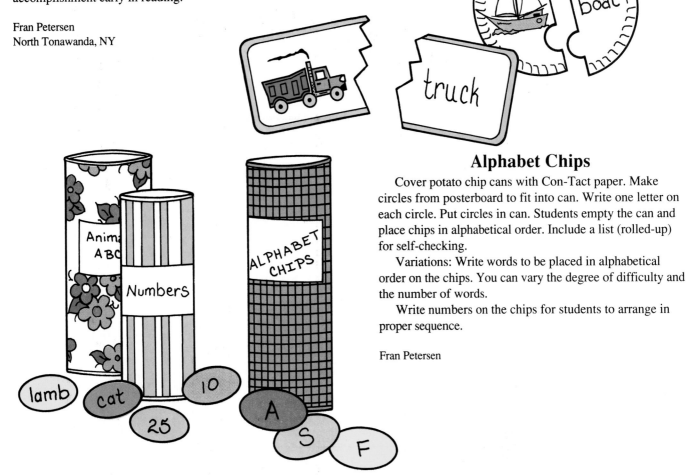

Alphabet Chips

Cover potato chip cans with Con-Tact paper. Make circles from posterboard to fit into can. Write one letter on each circle. Put circles in can. Students empty the can and place chips in alphabetical order. Include a list (rolled-up) for self-checking.

Variations: Write words to be placed in alphabetical order on the chips. You can vary the degree of difficulty and the number of words.

Write numbers on the chips for students to arrange in proper sequence.

Fran Petersen

Cap Capers

Save gallon milk carton caps or bleach caps to use as a versatile matching center. Trace around the cap on cardboard to make several circles and label with sets and numbers, colors and color words, or upper- and lowercase letters. Cut out and press inside lids. Code with matching stickers on the backs for self-checking.

Elaine Belscher
Spring Hill, FL

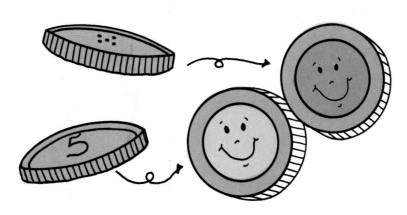

Spotlight on Centers

Holiday Dinner Activity

Practice following directions while you reinforce nutrition skills. Collect four of each of the following: plastic glasses, small paper plates, large paper plates, napkins, silverware. Cut out and laminate pictures of food from the four food groups, and store in a box with the dinnerware. Students use the chart to set the table, sort the food into groups on the large plates, and serve a balanced meal on each of the small plates.

Barbara Dixon
Loveland, OH

Shoelace Matchup

Clear acetate pockets and changeable program strips expand this center's skill possibilities. Punch seven holes alongside each pocket. Knot shoelaces in the left holes. Insert tagboard program strips in the pockets for a variety of matching activities—initial consonants, blends, homonyms, equivalent fractions.

Beverly Waddell
Dawson, GA

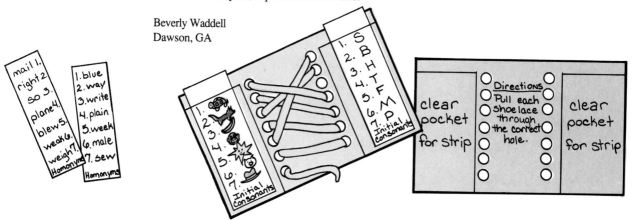

Fold-A-Flash-Card

Skill-building cards are easy to make. Cut out a triangle and fold as shown. Glue pictures on the three corners to use for rhyming. The student looks at the top picture, selects the rhyme, and then unfolds to check. He'll find a smiley face inside the flap if he's correct. Also good for vocabulary definitions and synonyms.

Margaret Maxwell
Oregon City, OR

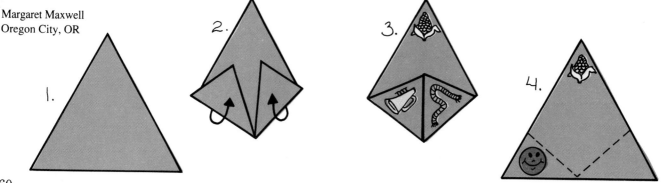

60

Freddie's Facts

Make a large frog for each student and label with any of these numbers: 1, 2, 3, 4, 5, 6, 8, 9, 10, 12, 15, 16, 18, 20, 24, 25, 30, 36. For a class bingo-type activity, roll a pair of dice and call out the numbers to the students. They multiply and cover up the totals with game chips. First to completely cover Freddie becomes the next caller. For an individual activity, follow this same procedure, but provide each student his or her own pair of dice.

Lynda Kinman
Hartford, AL

Circus String-A-Longs

This versatile learning center helps children with ABC order. Punch a hole in the side of a cut-out tent and attach a long piece of yarn. Cut 26 clowns, label from *a* to *z*, and punch a hole in the sides of each. Students string the clowns on the yarn in ABC order. Make additional sets of clowns labeled with numbers, story events, days of the week.

Elizabeth Cole
Annapolis, MD

The Ears Have It!

Make a series of cute bunnies as shown and write a numeral in each bunny's bow tie. Make many ears and draw different number sets on each. Students select two ears that will total the number on each rabbit. For a language arts center, try compound words or beginning sounds. For color recognition, make the ears the color of the color word on the bunny's tie.

Becky Hill
Great Bend, KS

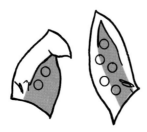

Turkey Addition

In the center of a small paper plate, draw a turkey's head and label with a plus sign and a number (+3, +6, etc.). Make ten construction paper feathers, write a number on each, and attach to the plate with a brad fastener. Students add the number on the feather to the number on the plate and flip to check. Feathers can be arranged at random so students can practice alone or in pairs.

Glenna Sternin
North Tonawanda, NY

Front

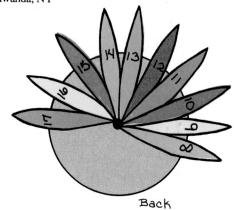

Back

Opposite Ends Of The Rainbow

Make a colorful matching center to brighten antonym practice! Color and cut out a tagboard rainbow as shown. Laminate. Label cut-out clouds with antonyms for students to match. Code the backs of the cutouts with numbers for self-checking.

Joan M. Wessels
Mason City, IA

Nothing Beats A Great Pair Of Legs

Use this large caterpillar for practice with initial and final consonants. Glue a picture word on each body segment; then make individual legs labeled with beginning and ending sounds. To work on place value, draw bundles of tens and ones on each segment. Children match numerals and place value words to the bundles.

Sister Mary Damien Buskirk
Mendham, NJ

Variation:

62

Look at the incomplete word on each ear of corn.
Decide which vowel combination will complete the word.
Place ear in correct basket.

Vowel Harvest

On a large sheet of poster board, draw a scarecrow surrounded by five bushel baskets. Label each basket with an *r*-controlled vowel (*ar, er, ir, or, ur*). Cut a slit at the top of each basket to serve as a pocket. Make many ears of corn from yellow construction paper. On each write a word missing its *r*-controlled vowel. Students place the ears in the correct baskets to form complete words. For self-correction, write the complete word(s) on the back of each ear. Variations: vowel sounds, parts of speech, math problems.

Mary Vander Poppen
Seattle, WA

Gone Fishin'

Print words on construction paper fish. Attach a paper clip at the mouth of each fish. Put them into a fishbowl. Use a small magnet attached to the end of the line of a small fishing pole. The "fisherman" keeps all the fish he knows. Fish for dinner!

Rachel Carter

Place Value French Fries

French fries, anyone? Place single tagboard french fries, as well as groups of ten, in fast-food french fry bags. Students count and record the number in each bag.

Connie Connely
Catoosa, OK

Vowel Hangars

Write words on jets, using short- and long-vowel sounds. Students must land the jets at the right hangar. Note: Each hangar should have a pocket or runway space to park jets.

Fran Petersen
North Tonawanda, NY

Raindrops

Draw a large umbrella on poster board. Make slits as indicated in illustration and insert paper clips. Make several sets of raindrops, each set a different color of construction paper. Write words on the raindrops. Students put words in alphabetical order by clipping them across the umbrella. Code the backs with numbers to indicate sequence for self-correction.

Interest Center Seminar display

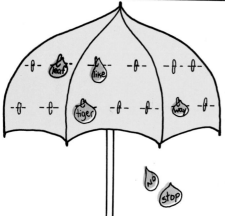

Study Bug

From blue poster board, cut eight to ten circles (about six-inch diameter). From black construction paper, cut two circles about the size of a quarter (eyes) and two antenna-shaped pieces. Glue the eyes and antennas to one circle. Laminate all pieces. In each of the circles except the face, make a slit large enough for a paper clip. Assemble shapes on a wall or bulletin board in the form of a caterpillar.

Cut a leaf shape from green construction paper large enough for a library card pocket and attach it near the Study Bug. Cut smaller pieces and program according to use. Store pieces in pocket.

Programming Suggestions:

— Write vocabulary words on small cards. Students arrange them in alphabetical order by slipping one card under a paper clip in each body segment.

— Print an upper- or lowercase letter on each segment. Write the matching letters on cards.

— Write a consonant or vowel on the segment. Card shows picture of object that begins or ends with the consonant or has the vowel sound.

— Print numeral on segment. Cards may have matching set, number word, number fact, or statement with missing addend.

— For science create a matching activity using inventions and inventors.

— Match states and capitals.

— Match fraction names and pictures or equivalent fractions.

Jenée Todd
Columbus, GA

Flip Paddle

For a sturdy holder for skill cards at centers, drill a hole on each side at the top of a wooden paddle. Put two loose-leaf rings through holes and attach flash cards.

Meg Hedrick
Abilene, TX

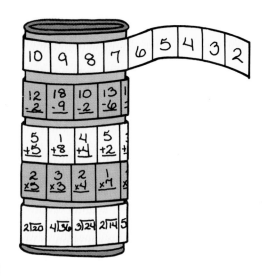

A New Twist

Here's a new twist to a Pringles can center. Cut five strips of lightweight paper to fit around the can. Program answers on the top strip and corresponding problems on the remaining four strips. Tape around the can so strips will turn easily. Students turn the strips to line up problems with a common answer. For best results, laminate the strips.

Elizabeth Cole
Annapolis, MD

Play Ball

Give each student a cut-out bat with a number or number word on it. Ask students to make cut-out baseballs to match their bats. Each ball must be another way to write the number on the bat.

Students may draw their bats and balls on paper or cut and paste. You may wish to place the bats in a learning center. As students cut out balls, they can leave them at the center for other students to manipulate and record. How about a contest? Who can make the most balls? The answers must be accurate to count.

Black Cat ABC

Cut out a picket fence and tape it to the side of a metal file cabinet. Label black cats with words to alphabetize and on the back of each, place a small piece of magnetic tape. The tape allows the children to rearrange the cats until they have the correct ABC order.

Shirley Liby
New Castle, IN

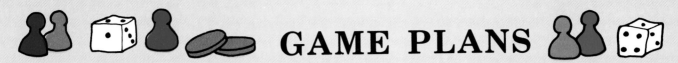

GAME PLANS

Spelling Game

Spelling reviews will no longer be humdrum with this game based on television's "Wheel of Fortune." Write each letter of a spelling word on a large piece of tagboard. Pick students to hold the letters with their backs to the class. When a player guesses a correct letter, the student holding that letter turns around and faces the class. If a player guesses a correct letter, he may guess another letter—or the whole word. Continue with more spelling words until interest flags.

Rebecca Gibson
Auburn, AL

A Whale Of A Job!

Make a large whale gameboard and label with vowels. Prepare a stack of word cards with missing vowels, and provide a different color of game chips for each player. Students take the top card and cover up a corresponding circle on the gameboard. First to play all his game chips wins!

Kay Atherton
Gaines, MI

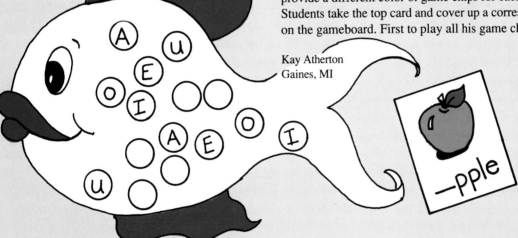

Bang!

Children will enjoy taking this game home to play with parents. Run off sheets of 2" x 2" squares on which sight words are written. A few squares are labeled simply, "Bang!" After cutting the squares apart, place them in a small container. Players take turns pulling out cards and reading them. They keep each card they read correctly, but return all incorrect ones. If the word "BANG!" is drawn, all the player's cards go back in the container. The person with the most cards at the end of five rounds wins.

Diana McGuckin
Kankakee, IL

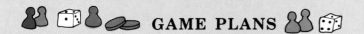

Ho-Ho-Holiday Games

How do you keep 30 excited children happy and busy at the annual class Christmas party? With these fun and easy-to-organize games, you and your students will enjoy the big event together.

Annette Mathias
Partridge, KS

Fill The Stocking

Divide the class into two to four teams, seated on the floor in rows, for this holiday relay. Give each team a large sock or stocking and four or five small items (pencil, eraser, ball, ruler, for example). To begin, the first player on each team fills his team's stocking with his items. The second player takes the stocking, upacks it, and hands it and the items to the next player to refill. The first team to move their stocking to the end of their line wins!

Stockings And Straws

Divide your class into two or more teams. Give each child a straw. Cut out a construction paper stocking for each team. To play, the first child on each team sucks up his team's stocking with his straw and puts it on the next child's desk. If the stocking falls on the floor, the player must pick it up with the straw, not with his hands. The team finishing first is the winner.

Snowball Through The Wreath

For a challenging game that's sure to please, hang a small jingle bell several inches from the center of a wreath. Suspend the wreath in your room. Tie an old white sock into a ball. Children try to throw the sock (the "snowball") through the center of the wreath to score a point. Award an extra point to students who also ring the bell with their throw.

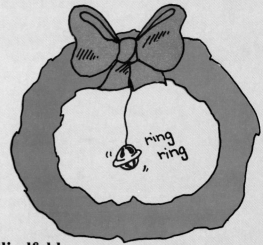

Merry Christmas Blindfold

Exchange holiday greetings with a giggle! Have students stand in a circle around one child, who is blindfolded and given a yardstick. The blindfolded child points to someone in the circle with the yardstick. The child pointed to takes the end of the yardstick and says, "Merry Christmas." The blindfolded child guesses the identity of the speaker. If correct, the two children switch places.

Lincoln Game

WHAT YOU NEED: Gameboard, 1 die, game pawns, answer key, and 20-25 cards with questions about Lincoln or any other subject.

HOW TO PLAY: In turn, player rolls a die, moves the number of spaces indicated, and picks up a question card. If he is able to answer the question correctly, he stays on that space. If he is unable to answer correctly, he goes back to his previous position. The first player to get Abe to the White House is the winner!

Joanne Rooney

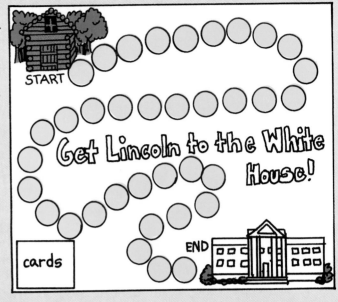

Get Lincoln to the White House!

START

END

cards

A Quick Spin For Math

Have children stand under numbers written on the chalkboard. Say any math fact. Children spin around if the answer is their number!

Judy Brisbine
Wessington Springs, SD

Find The Real Lemon!

Cut a slot in a lemonade mix can to hold the pieces for this game. Write correct and incorrect multiplication problems on lemon cutouts. Children put correct lemons in the can, then turn the can over to reveal an answer key on the bottom. Only incorrect lemons should be leftover and should match the answer key.

Ann Ballard
New Castle, IN

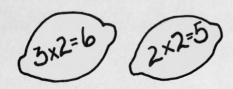

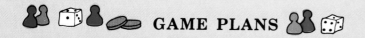
Host Ghost

Good listening skills make this game challenging and fun to play. Make a paper ghost. Have children sit in a circle, with one child, the Host Ghost, blindfolded and seated in the center. Pass the paper ghost around the circle. When the Host Ghost says, "Stop," the person holding the paper ghost gives out a moan. The Host Ghost tries to guess who moaned. If he guesses correctly, he stays in the center for another turn. If he does not, he must change places with the person holding the ghost. The new Host Ghost starts the play again.

Annette Mathias
Partridge, KS

Boo-hoo Ghosts

Get your reading groups in the haunting spirit! Label ghost cutouts with vocabulary words, labeling some with "Boo-hoo," and place in a box. Each child pulls ghosts from the box and reads the words until reaching a crying ghost. Then he passes the box on to the next child. Player with the most ghosts wins!

Patricia Bialaszewski
Dunkirk, NY

ABC Train

Play an ABC train game on the floor. Label engine and boxcar cards with words. Words written on engine cards should come before the other words alphabetically. Divide the class into teams. Give one player per team an engine card and all other players boxcar cards. On a signal, teams must arrange their cards in correct ABC order on the floor. First to do so wins!

Janet Hiller
Gary, IN

Nerf Ball Math

Use a Nerf football to provide math practice. With a permanent marker draw puzzle pieces all over the ball, and number each piece. When the child catches the football, he either adds or multiplies the numbers his thumbs are on. You can be "all thumbs" and still enjoy this game!

Sr. Annette Fiala
Waterloo, IA

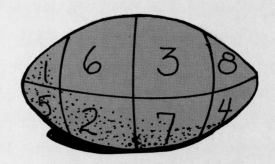

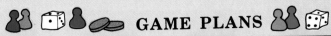

Career Checkers

A great way to give an old game a new look! Label every other square of a checker gameboard with a job description and list matching job titles on an answer key. Students play Career Checkers just like regular checkers, naming the occupation described or losing a turn.

Cheri Crockett
Kansas City, KS

Answer Key

1. Pilot	12. Baker	23. Lawyer
2. Nurse	13. Waiter—Waitress	24. Glassblower
3. Geologist	14. Farmer	25. Astronaut
4. Paleontologist	15. Police Officer	26. Astronomer
5. Actor—Actress	16. Mail Carrier	27. Teacher
6. Meteorologist	17. Barber—Beautician	28. Clerk
7. Dentist	18. Photographer	29. Custodian
8. Trash Collector	19. Artist	30. Cook—Chef
9. Auto Mechanic	20. Veterinarian	31. Disc Jockey
10. Carpenter	21. Fire fighter	32. Cowboy
11. Ichthyologist	22. Pharmacist	

The checkerboard grid contains the following clues:

1. I fly an airplane.
2. I help your doctor.
3. I study rocks and the earth.
4. I study dinosaurs and fossils.
5. You can see me on TV or in the movies.
6. I tell you what the weather will be like.
7. I work on your teeth.
8. I pick up trash and garbage.
9. I make sure your car runs right.
10. I can help build houses.
11. I study all about fish.
12. I bake bread and cookies.
13. I take your order in a restaurant.
14. I grow the food that you eat.
15. I catch criminals.
16. I bring you cards and letters.
17. I cut your hair.
18. I take pictures for a newspaper.
19. I paint pictures.
20. I take care of your pets when they are sick.
21. I put out fires.
22. I mix up the prescription the doctor gives you.
23. I can help you in court.
24. I make beautiful things from glass.
25. I can fly into space.
26. I study the stars.
27. I help you learn many things.
28. I take your money at the grocery store.
29. I clean schools and other buildings.
30. I make the meals you eat in a restaurant.
31. I play music for you on the radio.
32. I work on a ranch.

Take A Nibble

Give each child a paper cheese and write review words on paper mice. Children pronounce the words and punch a hole in their cheese for each correct pronunciation. The one with the most nibbles wins!

Betty Tipsword
Laurel Ridge, VA

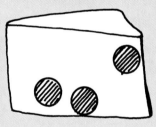

Tennis Ball Throw

Plan a "tennis match" that gives children practice in measuring. Have students stand behind a line four feet from the blackboard. Each student throws a ball covered with flour or chalk dust at the board, steps back one foot, and tries to hit the spot made by his first throw. The distance between the two marks is measured in inches. The closest hit wins. (Place newspaper on the floor to avoid flour or chalk marks.)

Grace Morina
Blackwood, NJ

Spelling Spots

To play Spelling Spots found on the next page, label playing cards with spelling words and place them in a stack on the gameboard. In turn, players draw a card and read it to their spelling partner, who tries to spell the word. If correct, the speller flips a coin to see how many spaces to move his marker: heads—one space, tails—two spaces. First to FINISH wins!

Janice Linkous
Martinsville, VA

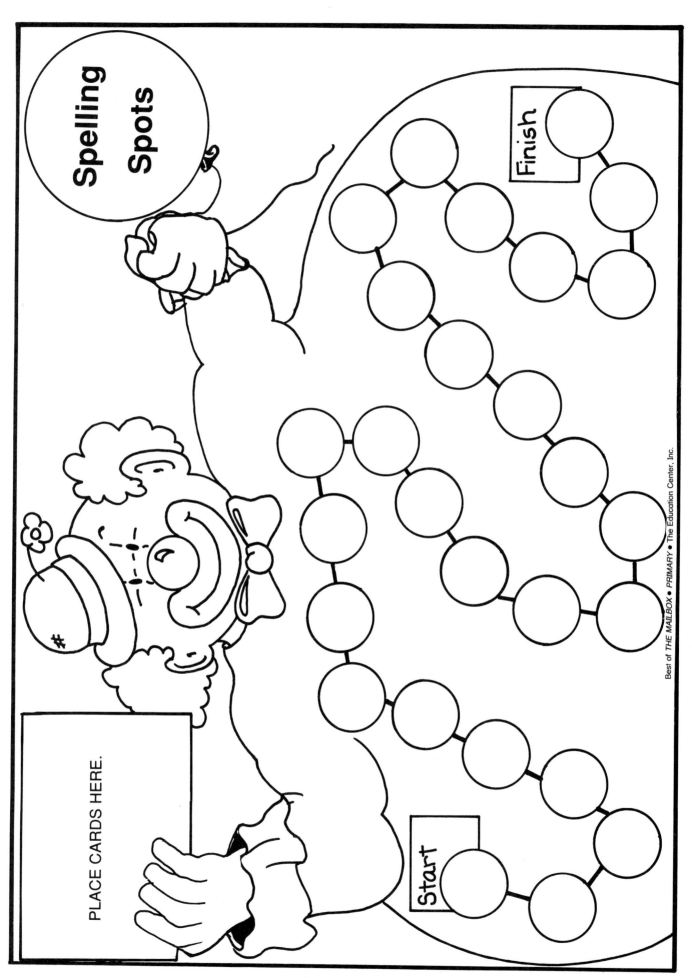

Note To Teacher: Use with "Spelling Spots" on page 71.

Love Is A Teddy Bear

Teddy Bear Fun

Here are the bare essentials for a week of teddy bear fun. Children will delight in a different activity each day. Love a bear today!

- Provide materials to make heart teddies, thumbprint teddies, stuffed paper teddies, or a tree of hearts and teddies.
- Trace bear outlines on one-inch graph paper and color checkered teddies.
- Assemble Teddy Books shaped like bears for creative writing.
- Decorate bookmarks using bear stickers and red hearts. Punch a hole in the top and add a piece of red yarn.
- Bake teddy bear cut-out cookies with red cinnamon hearts.
- For math practice, make flash cards in bear shapes.
- Design bear greeting cards using "bear" words and phrases such as:

unbearable	I can't bear to . . .	bare facts
bear paws	You bear a resemblance to . . .	bare necessities
bear hug	One of the bear essentials is . . .	bareback
bear up	Grin and bear it!	barefoot
bearskin	Get your bearings!	barefaced
bear claws	Bear this in mind . . .	barely visible

Nancy McDevitt
Reading, PA

Stuffed Animal Pen Pals

Primary students enjoy their first letter-writing experience when they write letters to and get answers from stuffed animals. Bring one or two animals to school, name them, and make a mailbox for their letters. After students have mailed their questions, write an answer to each student from the animal. Really encourages creativity!

Pamela Duke
Lompoc, CA

Teddy In The Tub

Make 12 teddy bears. Write a word on each bear, some with short vowels and some with long vowels. Laminate for durability. Students sort the bears into the appropriate tub. Provide an answer key to make this self-checking.

Cory Mikkelson
Monticello, MN

Our Family Tree

National Grandparents Day—First Sunday After Labor Day

With your class, make friends with a nursing home resident. Prepare the students ahead of time by discussing the needs of the elderly. Make gifts, write letters, send tapes, visit with small groups.

A special senior will appreciate this quilt wall-hanging made by your students. Have each child decorate a six-inch square of felt with paint, yarn, buttons, etc. Sew the finished squares together and bind the edges. This makes a nice thank-you gift or present for a local nursing home.

Contact your local council on aging to arrange for senior citizens to serve in your classroom as volunteers. Not only do they have valuable services to offer to you and your students, but they also derive much-needed feelings of self-esteem and worth. Everyone wins in this situation!

Narrow the generation gap! Have your students interview their favorite senior citizen to discover what everyday life was like a generation ago:
- Favorite pastimes
- School
- Chores
- Music
- Dress
- Family rules

For a quick thought exercise, ask your students to make two lists:
- What's good about being a grandparent?
- What's bad about being a grandparent?

A "Yesterday's Yummies" cookbook is a nice take-home gift as well as a real learning experience. Children ask grandparents or other senior friends for the recipe for a food they ate when they were young. In class, the students organize the recipes and prepare ditto masters for the cookbook. Discuss how food preparation and eating habits have changed. Students will enjoy making some of the dishes to share in the class.

Make "This Is Your Life" viewers to present to grandparents. On adding machine tape, children draw scenes from their grandparents' lives in chronological order. Cut matching slits in paper plates and thread the strips through to show one scene at a time.

Beanbag It!

Activities using beanbags are excellent opportunities for developing body awareness in young children. They provide practice in improving throwing and catching skills and eye-hand coordination. Karen Adams Stone of West Elementary School in Goodland, KS, uses the following individual and partner activities to explore body movements with her children. These routines utilize all body parts and can also be used as relays.

INDIVIDUAL ACTIVITIES

1. Arms
A. Toss upward and catch. One hand, both hands, backs of hands.
B. Toss overhead, turn, and catch.
C. Toss upward, turn completely around, and catch.
D. Toss upward, touch the floor, and catch.
E. Toss forward, run and catch.
F. Toss overhead from one side to the other.

2. Legs
A. Balance beanbag on instep. Walk, hop, swing leg forward and back with bag balanced on instep.
B. Toss to self from toe. From knee. From heel.
C. Place beanbag on both feet and toss to self.
D. Place beanbag between feet and toss to self.
E. Place beanbag between feet and jump several times.

3. Arms, Legs, Trunk
A. From lying-on-back position, toss to self from various arm positions. Toss bag to self from toe. From feet.
B. Using both feet, bring beanbag overhead and deposit in back of head. Try bringing it up and depositing to the side.

4. Head
A. With beanbag on head, walk, run, skip, hop, or jump without losing bag.
B. Toss bag forward from head to hands. Toss sideways and catch. Toss backward. Toss beanbag for distance from head.

5. Body
A. From a standing position, throw beanbag into the air. Sit down quickly and catch.
B. Begin in sitting position, throw, and stand up and catch. Repeat with a lying-down sequence.
C. Try juggling with two bags. Try with three bags.
D. With beanbag balanced on head, sit down, and get up. Lie down and get up.
E. With the beanbag pressed between the knees, hop like a kangaroo.

PARTNER ACTIVITIES

1. Toss back and forth using different types of throws—right hand, left hand, under leg, around back, etc.
2. Toss with beanbag balanced on head, elbow, and knee.
3. With back to partner, take bunny hop position. Kick bag back to partner.
4. A. Using two bags at a time, each holds a bag. Throw bags back and forth at the same time.
   B. Try tossing both bags at the same time, using various means of throwing.
   C. Try keeping three bags moving between two people.

Halloween is a perfect time to introduce beanbag activities to your class. Karen uses these easy-to-make beanbags as party favors, too.

Christmas 2003

'Twas the night before Christmas and on our asteroid,
Not a creature was stirring not even a droid.
The space socks were hung by the instrument panel,
Socks of helium, plastic, and 3 percent flannel.

The children were nestled in pressurized cots,
Dreaming of space toys and programmed robots.
Milon Mama and I set the spaceship on cruise
And we just settled down for a long winter's snooze.

When out on the landing bay we heard such a clatter
I jumped from my pod to see what was the matter.
I couldn't believe what could make all that racket
So I flipped on the radar and started to track it.

When what to my wondering eyes should appear
But a jet-propelled sleigh and eight weightless reindeer.
The next picture came—a three-second delay —
Then I saw Santa Skywalker driving the sleigh.

He was wearing a pressurized suit of bright red
With an aerospace helmet on top of his head.
In the back of his sleigh with his bag full of toys
A computer printout listed good girls and boys.

Santa hastened to open our ship's starboard hatch
And tossed down some goodies—there was quite a batch—
A doll that said, "Blast Off," a time warp chess set,
A laser-run top, an electronic pet.

He followed the toys in—a straight drop down the chute—
With a clink and a clank of each magnetic boot.
He stuffed all the stockings, trimmed our synthetic tree,
And arranged all the packages, neat as could be.

Then he took a quiet look at our charted projection
To see if our course met his inspection.
I guess he approved of our going that way
'Cause he nodded and beamed himself back to the sleigh.

Then he took off through space with his reindeer and pack,
Leaving my radar to bleep and go black.
But our video scanner showed his message unfurled,
"Sure hope your Christmas is out of this world."

Margo Schullerts
Yuba City, CA

A Black American Who Made History

Celebrate Black History Month in February with ideas that introduce young children to the accomplishments of this famous black American.
Sharon Haley

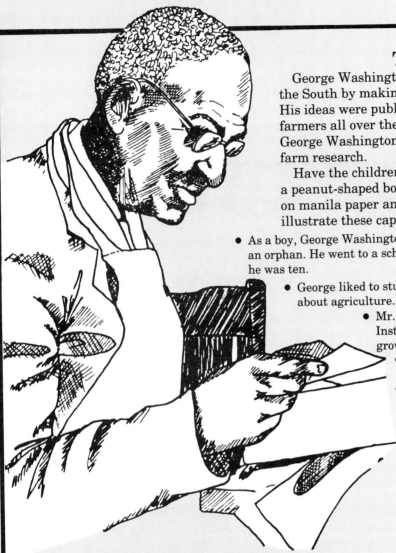

The Peanut Man

George Washington Carver helped to change the economy of the South by making it less dependent on cotton production. His ideas were published by the Department of Agriculture for farmers all over the world. He donated his life savings to the George Washington Carver Foundation which continues his farm research.

Have the children write about George Washington Carver in a peanut-shaped booklet. Children can trace two peanut shapes on manila paper and cut them out for covers. Have students illustrate these captions:

- As a boy, George Washington Carver was a slave and an orphan. He went to a school for black children when he was ten.
- George liked to study plants. He went to college to learn about agriculture.
- Mr. Carver became a teacher and scientist at Tuskegee Institute in Alabama. He found ways to make plants grow bigger and better.
- He invented many uses for the peanut, sweet potato, and soybean.
- His work has helped farmers all over the world.

Sweet Potato Days

Remember George Washington Carver every day. Bring in sweet potatoes for children to root in water. These grow quickly in a sunny window. As they watch their plants grow during the year, children will be reminded of this famous black American.

Peanut Butter

Have students make peanut butter using the following recipe. Children may copy the recipe and add it to their peanut booklets:

1 c. unsalted, roasted peanuts
½ tsp. salt
2–3 Tbsp. vegetable oil

1. Put all ingredients in a blender container.
2. Blend for one minute.
3. Eat right away!

(Homemade peanut butter will not last as long as the kind you buy at the store.)

BOOKMAKING!

YOU WILL NEED:

2 pieces of cardboard—7" x 9" each
1 piece of 2" wide masking tape—12" long
2 pieces of wallpaper or Con-Tact paper—
8" x 11" each
10 sheets of 8½" x 14" white mimeograph
paper
2 sheets of 8½" x 14" construction paper
1 large needle   sewing thread
1 awl or ice pick   scissors   glue

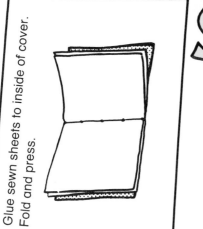

4. Glue sewn sheets to inside of cover. Fold and press.

You can use your book for:
- a scrapbook
- a gift for a parent or friend
- your original stories
- your autobiography
- an address and phone book
- a photo album
- a diary or journal

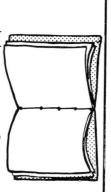

3. Place 10 sheets of 8½" x 14" paper on top of 2 sheets of 8½" x 14" construction paper. Fold. Punch 5 holes at fold. Sew through holes and through construction paper. Tie knot.

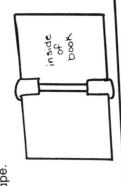

1. Place 2 pieces of 7" x 9" board on top of 12" piece of tape. Leave ½" between boards. Turn down excess tape.

inside of book

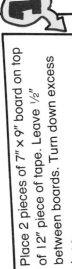

2. Cover backs of boards with 2 pieces of Con-Tact paper 8" x 11". Turn over. Trim corner edges diagonally. Turn down edges.

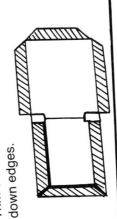

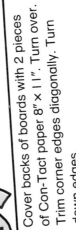

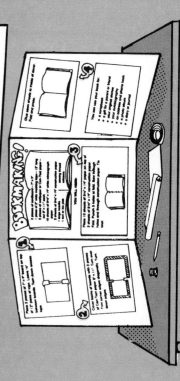

Use three large pieces of cardboard (about 20" x 20") from an old box to make your backdrop for this activity center. Paint the cardboard or cover with construction paper. Place all needed materials on the table in front of it.

Idea by Bill DeLeeuw
Interest Center Seminar Display

78

Party
Refreshment Centers

At these eight, fun centers, small groups of students make their own party treats. When each group has completed all centers, their plates are full.

Ask mother volunteers to help at centers, or display directions and samples for students to work alone. Divide the class into small groups and plan how to rotate groups through centers. Designate a signal for moving from one center to the next.

Dianne Kinard, Westminster, SC

Fancy Sandwiches

Meat spread, egg salad, or cheese spread can be used for decorative sandwiches. Use cookie cutters to cut sandwiches into special shapes.

Tasty Beverages

With an instant drink mix, groups can make pitchers of drinks, or each child can make a cup.

Decorated Cupcakes

At this center, have prepared cupcakes and icing, jelly beans, coconut, sprinkles, and candies. Each student designs a unique cupcake.

Jell-O Salad Egg on Coconut

Have each child blow out an egg the day before. When the yolk is out, wash egg and dip the end with the smaller hole in melted paraffin, or tape it to seal.

Then the class makes several flavors of this mixture, fills the empty shells, and refrigerates them overnight.

I 3-oz. pkg. Jell-O	I egg
I cup boiling water	½ cup milk

Dissolve Jell-O in water. Beat egg and milk together, and add to Jell-O at room temperature. One batch fills about 7–8 eggs.

On the party day, students peel these eggs for glossy, tasty Easter egg treats. At this station, each child shakes coconut and food coloring in a small container, puts it on his plate, and sets a Jell-O egg on top.

Hors D'Oeuvres Cutouts

Give each child a slice of cheese. He uses Tupperware hors d'oeuvre cutters to cut enough fancy cheese shapes to put on several crackers.

Fresh Vegetables and Dip

Here children peel their own carrots, slice radishes, and cut up celery and cauliflower. Adult supervision is needed at this center due to the use of paring knives and peelers. Also provide ingredients for dip so that each group can prepare a small serving.

Egg Dyeing

Provide hard-boiled eggs for students to dye. Color eggs with standard, food coloring dyes, or dip Q-tips in paint. Vinegar added to dyes creates more intense colors. If desired, offer wax crayons or decals for decorations.

Instant Pudding

The mess is worth the fun as children read and follow directions to make pudding. Have ingredients, utensils, and plastic cups ready. Each group makes a box of pudding and divides it equally into plastic cups.

Let's Go Out!

Give in to that "spring fever" and get outside with your kids for some fresh-air games!

Reverse Ball Relay

Running and passing make this an exciting relay with a reverse twist. Divide the class into columns of five to six players. Each player in the column is given a number. Place a ball about five feet in front of each column; then call a number. The player with that number from each column runs to the front, picks up the ball, and gives it to the first person in the column. He then resumes his original position to assist in passing the ball to the back. The ball may not be passed over his spot without being handled by him. When the ball reaches the back of the column, the direction is reversed. After handling the ball again, the player who was called runs to the front to receive the last pass. He replaces the ball in its starting place before returning to his own position. First team to complete the relay wins.

Kathy Pattak

Balloon Bounce

Split the class into two teams, and provide each with a sheet and a balloon. Teams spread out around the sheet and grasp it by the edges, placing balloons in the centers. After practicing tossing the balloons up and catching them, teams are ready to pass them from sheet to sheet, or toss one balloon up to let the other team catch. Teams can compete to see how many times they can bounce the balloon without stopping. See what suggestions your kids might add!

Sheet Chute

Sew two old sheets together and you'll have a parachute the kids will love to exercise with. Have them grab on all around, then walk, hop, and run in a circle. Play "The Sheet Says" just like "Simon Says" and give directions to sit, stand, and jump for a healthy workout.

Shoot The Rapids

Teams try to "shoot the rapids" by dodging balls on their way "downstream." Divide the class into three teams. Teams #1 and #2 line up on opposite sides of an imaginary river with two or three lightweight balls. Team #3 members stand at one end and wait for the signal to run the river. On a signal, they try to run to the opposite end, while those with balls (rapids) try to hit them. When hit, a runner stands behind a thrower. After several runs, rotate teams. To vary, have runners use another locomotor skill. Have throwers use nondominant hands or throw yarn balls.

Kathy Pattak
Pittsburgh, PA
1985

Roundup

Select a "farmer" to whisper three different animal names to students. Players spread apart, shut their eyes, then try to locate their mates by making the appropriate animal sounds. They link hands as they find all the members of their group.

Scoop Ball

To improve students' hand-eye coordination and basic catching skill, use homemade scoops. The scoops can be made in two sizes from gallon or ½-gallon milk jugs. Cut the scoops as illustrated. You can obtain free tennis balls from a private tennis court.

Students can use scoops in any of these ways:

1. Throw the ball up in the air and catch the ball with the scoop.
2. Bounce the ball against a wall and catch it with the scoop.
3. Throw the ball to each other with the hand and catch with the scoop.
4. With a partner, take turns throwing a ball and catching it in a scoop.
5. Start with the large scoop and progress to the smaller scoop.

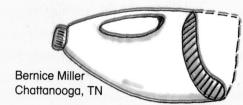

Bernice Miller
Chattanooga, TN

Sylvester and the Magic Pebble

Sylvester and the Magic Pebble COPYRIGHT © 1969 by William Steig. Reprinted by permission of Simon & Schuster, Inc.

Here's a read-aloud Caldecott Medal book that will spark children's imaginations. Follow up the story with these activities for creative dramatics, writing, and thinking. Good luck!

Lucky Me!

Sylvester was unlucky when it came to wishing on his magic pebble. Remind students that Sylvester made some unwise choices. Because he panicked, his last wish turned him into a rock! Ask children what they would do if they had three wishes. Caution them to think carefully!

Continue the good-luck theme by having children illustrate some common good-luck charms. Rabbits' feet, four-leaf clovers, rainbows, eyelashes, stars, and horseshoes are often credited with bringing good luck. Ask each child to choose a good-luck charm to include in an original story about "The Luckiest Day of My Life."

When You Wish Upon a Star

After Sylvester was rescued by his parents, they decided to put the magic pebble in a safe. Since Sylvester and his family were so happy to be together again, they didn't need to wish for anything else. Ask children if they would have locked the pebble away and why. Discuss responsibilities of having special powers or knowledge.

Discuss Sylvester's feelings of loneliness and helplessness, and his parents' feeling of sorrow. Then ask children to think of situations when they have felt powerless as Sylvester did when he was unable to change back into a donkey. Other books that deal with making wishes come true are *The Amazing Bone* by William Steig, *The Whingdingdilly* by Bill Peet, and *The Golden Touch* by Paul Galdone.

Your Wish Is My Command!

Make a list of students' wishes to compare. Lead children to the conclusion that some things we wish for are things we need while others are things we just want. Divide the class list into needs and wants.

Ask students to think about what would happen if our every wish were granted by a genie in a magic bottle. Have children role-play or write about situations with the genie such as:

I wish I could be a rock star.　　　I wish I never had to go to school.
I wish I could stay in bed all day.　　I wish everything I touched turned into gold.

"Stone Age" Art

Have children make unusual rock people or pebble pets. Provide yarn for students to wrap rocks or pebbles, leaving spaces to paint on faces or glue on wiggle eyes. Then have children create dioramas as settings to display their rocks. How about the Rock Family at Home or Pebble Pups on Parade for "Stone Age" art?

Sylvester's Pebbles

For practice in addition and subtraction, have children collect smooth, round pebbles. Provide small plastic containers for younger students to sort the pebbles by size, color, or appearance. Label task cards with addition and subtraction facts, and place them with the pebbles at a learning station. (For example: 7 pink pebbles + 5 black pebbles = ?) Vary this activity for older students by writing word problems on task cards.

The Daily Quack

Circle each error.
Copy the sentences correctly.

1. baby mallards cannot fly.

2. it takes a few weeks for their feathers to grow

3. There are three kinds of feathers

4. Down helps keep the babies warm

5. body feathers later cover their bodies.

6. flight feathers are large feathers that help the birds fly

7. Until their feathers grow in, ducks escape enemies by going into water.

8. they can swim soon after they hatch

Make Way For Ducklings

Students will enjoy this charming story of a mallard family and a policeman's aid in their city survival. Try out these activities based on Robert McCloskey's book, *Make Way For Ducklings*.

Sylvia Foust
Long Beach, NC

Ducky Motivation

KEEP YOUR DUCKS IN A ROW

ROW 1   Mary   Billy   Eva   Irene

ROW 2   Jason   C.J.   Julie   Lizzie   Teresa

ROW 3   Rod   Ted   Todd

Mrs. Mallard was the best at keeping ducklings in line. Try this management bulletin board to motivate students toward super conduct! Post ducks in rows corresponding to your seating arrangement. Children keep their ducks in place by following classroom rules. Throw a "quacker" party at the end of a set time period to reward "ducky" behavior.

Bird Food

A mallard's diet consists of more than peanuts. Provide resource materials so students can discover other food sources. Discuss what happens when wild birds are fed by people and become dependent on them. Will the birds that normally migrate follow their instincts or remain for handouts?

Mallard Manual

Table of Contents
Swimming and Diving
Walking in a Line
Coming When Called
Avoiding Things with Wheels

Mrs. Mallard did such a wonderful job of caring for her eight ducklings that all of the other mother mallards wanted her to write a book. Mrs. Mallard decided to call her book *Everything You Wanted To Know About Raising Ducklings*. Pick a chapter from the table of contents and write what you think she would have written.

Patricia McGuckin
Mesa, AZ

Wild Ducks

To discuss ducks in the wild, arrange for a visit by the local wildlife commissioner, game warden, or county extension agent. Help students prepare questions beforehand in order to use their visitor's time most effectively.

The Biggest Bear

Teacher Suggestions: Have children write a tall tale, spelling words, or a poem; or program worksheet with math problems. Use with activity on page 85.

The Biggest Bear

Johnny wanted a bearskin but found a pet that was a trial and tribulation to the residents of the valley. Read this humorous Caldecott Medal winner by Lynd Ward with your students, and discover how the Biggest Bear caused big trouble. See the worksheets on pages 84 and 86.

Bear Tracks

Put students on the track of sentence practice. Write these bear facts without capitals and punctuation on cut-out paw prints. Place in a path around the room. Have children re-write the sentences using capitals and correct punctuation.

—Bears eat fruit, roots, honey, insects, fish, and meat.
—Most bears can climb trees.
—Bears can swim well.
—Bears can run as fast as 35 miles per hour!
—Bears hibernate in caves or in holes in the ground.
—Do bears live alone?
—Cubs stay with their mothers about one year.
—The Kodiak bear is the biggest bear.

A Bear in the Orchard

Grandpa Orchard came upon a bear in the apple orchard. He ran for his life saying, "Better a bear in the orchard than an Orchard in the bear." What would your students do if they met a bear? Have children create a fanciful dialogue or write more practical suggestions.

cl ___   bl ___
fl ___   gl ___

Bearskin Bragging

Johnny wanted to brag about a bearskin on his barn. For a fun creative writing activity, ask students to create some outrageous, make-believe brags. Children can write their brags on duplicated bearskins using the pattern on page 84.

Bears in the Wild

The Biggest Bear did not want to return to the woods. Discuss what happens to wild animals who become dependent upon people for food. Park rangers often trap begging bears who frequent garbage dumps or threaten campers. When released elsewhere, they may be unable to fend for themselves. Some, like the Biggest Bear, end up in zoos. Have students design posters advocating protection of wildlife as humans encroach upon their territory.

Maple Sugar Surprise

One whiff of maple sugar sent the Biggest Bear tearing off in search of his favorite treat. Discuss how maple sugar is obtained from sap tapped from maple trees. Try this experiment for a maple sugar surprise. Boil maple syrup until thick and foamy. Spoon onto pans of clean, packed snow or crushed ice. When syrup turns waxy, twist it up onto a Popsicle stick for chewy, maple leather known as "sugar on snow."

Bear Blends

Johnny left his bear eating blueberries on the blueberry bluff. Use the pattern to make a tagboard bear and wheel for blend practice. Attach wheel with a brad. Children turn the wheel and write new blend words.

The Bear Facts

Compare the biggest bears.
Read the chart.
Write your answers on your own paper.

North American Bears

Name	brown bear (Kodiak and grizzly)	black bear
Color	yellow-brown to nearly black	light brown to black, light brown nose
Size	9 feet 700–1,600 lbs.	6 feet 250–500 lbs.
Where they live	south coast of Alaska, western United States	Canada, Alaska, U.S. mountains, Great Lakes, Gulf Coast
How they look	flat nose, light-tipped "grizzled" fur	straight nose
Facts	don't climb well, eat salmon in season	most widespread and numerous

1. Which bear is most widespread?
2. Which is the biggest bear?
3. What color is the brown bear?
4. Where do the Kodiak and grizzly live?
5. How much does the black bear weigh?
6. Which bear stands nine feet tall?
7. Are both bears found in Alaska?
8. Which bear cannot climb well?

Clifford The Big Red Dog

Enjoy reading about a huge, lovable dog and his friend in this popular book by Norman Bridwell. Then share these activities with your class.

Sylvia Foust
Long Beach, NC

Doggie Tales

Give creative story writing a different twist! Post these canine topics and instruct students to write and draw cartoons for any two. A good brainstorming session beforehand will help them come up with ideas in addition to those shown by Clifford.

The Day My Dog Went Camping
How to Wash a Dog
My Dog Loves Cats
A Good Watchdog Will . . .
The Games Dogs Play

Chow Down!

According to Emily Elizabeth, a dog like Clifford eats and drinks a lot! Use a dog food bag to provide some heavyweight math practice. Base questions on the feeding chart found on the back. Specify breed size (toy, medium, extra large), weight of dog, and number of feedings to find out how many cups certain dogs would eat daily.

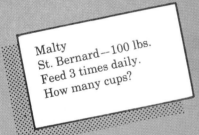

Malty
St. Bernard—100 lbs.
Feed 3 times daily.
How many cups?

Top Dogs

Find out who's "top dog" in your class! See how many students know the meanings of these phrases.

dog paddle
dog days
dog-eared
dog tags
underdog
hot dog

dog tired
dogfight (battle between air aces)
You're in the doghouse.
Let sleeping dogs lie.
You can't teach an old dog new tricks.

Doggie Biscuits

Like a lot of dogs, Clifford would sit up and beg for a biscuit. Discuss how rewards help animals learn tricks. Then serve up a version of "doggie biscuits" for a reading comprehension and sequencing activity! Write individual recipe steps on bone-shaped cutouts, coding backs for self-checking of sequence. Place a laminated copy of the recipe along with the cutouts in a real mixing bowl.

Doggie Biscuits:

¼ cup shortening
⅓ cup shredded cheddar cheese
2 cups biscuit mix
⅔ cup milk

Preheat oven to 425 degrees. Stir the shortening and cheese into the biscuit mix. Add the milk. Stir together with a fork. Beat 15 strokes. Grease a cookie sheet. Drop the mix by tablespoonfuls onto the sheet. Put the biscuits in the oven. Remove after 12–15 minutes.

Clifford's Sweaters

Clifford has a wardrobe of sweaters to teach colors. Make a large, red Clifford on poster board. Cut out and laminate. Cut out a sweater for each color. Have children dress Clifford with the sweater in the color of the day. To extend the use of sweaters, label with days of the week, months, or number words.

Retha Mancil
Ozark, AL

Bedtime For Frances

Every child can identify with Frances' attempts to delay bedtime. In this story the bedtime monsters and noises in the night disappear when Frances faces her fears of the dark. Read *Bedtime for Frances* by Russell Hoban with your children, and try these follow-up activities.

Sleepyheads

Badgers are hibernating animals. Display pictures of some animals that hibernate in winter. Talk about steps necessary for winter survival of these and other animals. Have students write a paragraph from the point of view of a badger just emerging from his winter burrow, or a groundhog on Groundhog Day, February 2.

Excuses, Excuses . . .

Frances could think of lots of excuses to stay up later. Discuss her fears of the dark. How did she conquer them after reassurances from Father and the threat of a spanking? Have students write and illustrate ridiculous excuses to complete the sentence, "I can't go to bed because . . ."

Alarm Clock For Frances

Use an old alarm clock or a large clock cutout with moveable hands to provide practice in telling time. Have children set the hands to the times shown on Frances' daily schedule. Provide answers on the back of schedule for self-checking.

Frances' Day

Wake Up—7:00	Snacktime—3:00
Breakfast—7:15	Play with Friends—3:30
School—8:00	Suppertime—6:00
Lunchtime—12:00	Bedtime for Frances—8:00
Dismissal—2:30	

Bedtime Delay Tactics

Discuss Frances' bedtime preparations. Have children compare their own bedtime routine, including stories, snacks, songs, prayers, kisses, and soft cuddlies. List Frances' bedtime steps on sentence strips, and have children sequence them in the correct order.

Frances drank a glass of milk.
Father gave Frances a piggyback ride.
Frances kissed Mother and Father.
Frances asked for her teddy bear and doll.
Frances asked for another kiss.
Frances wanted the door open.
Mother and Father said, "Goodnight."

Frances' Listening Center

Frances heard a strange noise at her window that excited her imagination. Stimulate your students' imagination at this listening center. Tape familiar sounds for children to identify at a listening center. Provide tapes of varied music or sounds, and have students imagine and illustrate movie scenes for the sound track. As a class make up an alphabet song like Frances sang at bedtime. Have the class sing their song to a familiar tune and tape-record it.

Discovery Center

Set up a Badger Discovery Center to acquaint children with badgers. Have students find out about their physical characteristics, habitat, food, and life cycle.

- Share these facts in the *Badger Bulletin,* a newsletter written and illustrated by the class.
- Show tracks made by badgers and compare to other animals.
- Model burrows and tunnels with clay.
- Display food eaten by badgers. Show seeds, fruit, eggs, berries, nuts, acorns, earthworms, or insects.
- Borrow a caged badger, raccoon, opossum, mouse, or squirrel for a short classroom visit.

Underground Real Estate

European badgers live in groups called *clans.* Together they make underground networks of rooms and tunnels. Many generations of badgers have enlarged the networks. Have children draw a map of a badger's imaginary underground home, label rooms, and write a real estate ad for the *Badger Bulletin.* Read about other underground inhabitants in books about rabbits, rats, snakes, prairie dogs, moles, and weasels.

A Pocket For Corduroy

Here's a sampling of activities your younger children will enjoy after hearing Don Freeman's *A Pocket For Corduroy*.

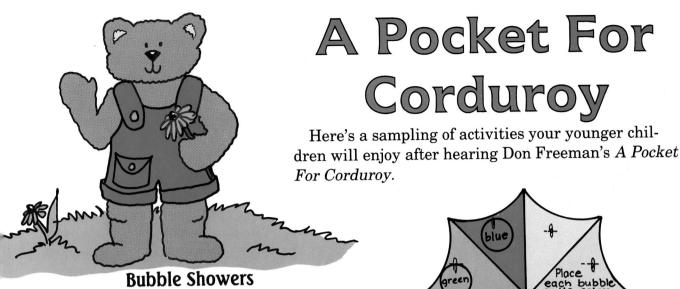

Bubble Showers

Bubble Showers will be just the thing to teach color words. Enlarge, cut out, and color the umbrella. Then cut slits along dotted lines and insert paper clips as shown. After labeling bubble cutouts with color words, laminate for durability.

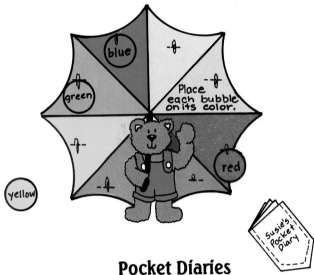

Please Feed The Bear!

Here's a true-false activity guaranteed to tempt students. Form a pocket by stapling half of a paper plate to a whole plate. Label cut-out cards with statements based on any story your students have read. Children place only the true statements in the pocket. Use for math facts, long or short vowels.

Pocket Diaries

Make minidiaries to practice neatness, handwriting, and following directions! Staple enough 4″ × 5″ pages together for a one-week period and cover with construction paper. After labeling pages with days, have students record daily chores at school or home.

Pocket Tachistoscope

There's a hole in this pocket! Program several paper strips for a multipurpose tachistoscope. Students pull up strips to check their answers.

Sylvia Foust

Sorting Practice Pockets

These pockets for Corduroy will dress up any sorting practice! Label pockets for vowel sounds, math facts, or classification. Provide cut-out cards to match the skills.

What Is It?

Patricia McGuckin of Mesa, Arizona, suggests using library card pockets for this cut-and-paste activity. After reading *A Pocket For Corduroy*, ask children to cut out magazine pictures of objects that would fit into a pocket. Have each child write a description of his object without naming it. Then paste descriptions on the pocket fronts and place cutouts inside. Keep all the pockets in a center. Students read each other's descriptions, guess what's in the pocket, and check by looking inside.

Sam, Bangs, And Moonshine

Sam has a difficult time separating fantasy from reality until she learns the consequences of talking "moonshine." Because of her tall tales, a friend and her cat named Bangs get into serious trouble.

Read this Caldecott Award winner by Evaline Ness with your class, and create some moonshine fun with these activities.

Let's Talk To The Animals

Sam talked to her cat, Bangs, and Bangs talked back! Many pet-owners speak to their pets, but most animals can only answer non-verbally. Discuss how animals communicate with each other and with humans. What behavior do animals demonstrate when they are angry, curious, fearful, playful, courting, or establishing their territories?

Margaret—Peggy, Marge
Susan—Susie, Sue
Rebecca—Becky
Elizabeth—Beth, Liz
Virginia—Ginny
Samantha—Sam
Amanda—Mandy
Kathleen—Kate, Kathy
Andrew—Andy
James—Jimmy
Joseph—Joey
William—Billy, Will
John—Johnny, Jack
Robert—Bobbie, Rob
Ronald—Ronnie, Ron
Abigail—Abby

Such Foolishness!

Sam's father says that "moonshine" spells trouble. Moonshine is his word for talking nonsense or making up tall tales. Here are some fun synonyms for foolishness that will make children giggle. Have students divide words into syllables or circle double consonants.

nonsense	horsefeathers	bunkum
foolishness	folly	bunk
humbug	malarkey	flummery
claptrap	fiddle-faddle	hokum
chatter	gobbledegook	applesauce
chitchat	gibberish	rubbish
jabber	babble	baloney
garbage	drivel	flapdoodle
		flummadiddle

Short Stuff

Sam's real name is Samantha, but she's always called Sam. Have children with nicknames tell their real names and how they got their nicknames. Make a classroom list of nicknames, or have children write the familiar forms of these proper names and alphabetize them.

Gerbils Versus Baby Kangaroos

When her father brought home a furry, little creature that hopped, Sam thought it was a baby kangaroo. Compare gerbils to kangaroos. Why would one make a better pet than the other? Gerbils are odorless, gentle, friendly, curious little rodents. They make excellent classroom pets for scientific observation and entertainment.

Sea Creatures

Mermaids are beautiful sea creatures mentioned in tales of the ocean. Perhaps Sam had heard of them because her father was a fisherman. Sam created a mermaid mother who lived in a cave on Blue Rock. Have children imagine and draw other creatures in King Neptune's undersea world or act out a conversation with Charlie the Tuna.

A Pocketful Of Cricket

Jay collects nature's little wonders in his pockets. On the first day of school, he arrives with a pocketful of Cricket. Read *A Pocketful of Cricket* by Rebecca Caudill with your class and share these activities.

Classroom Cricket

Crickets make fascinating easy-to-care-for pets in the classroom. Look for crickets in moist areas under rocks or decaying wood. Keep a cricket in a mesh-covered fishbowl or glass jar with a few inches of soil and some leaves. Sprinkle leaves with water and provide bread, lettuce, or bonemeal dog biscuits as cricket food.

Crickets "fiddle" in the dark. Observe together how crickets make their noise, and have children compare this to playing a fiddle.

First Day Of School

Jay decided to take his friend Cricket to school for security, but Cricket became an embarrassment. Discuss how Jay felt on his way to school and how Cricket helped him to overcome his shyness. Ask children to talk about their first-day fears, and plan a special sharing time. To help classmates get acquainted, ask them to bring in one special thing to share.

Wash Day Surprises

On wash days, mothers take care to empty pockets before putting clothes in the washing machine. Children's pockets often contain unusual surprises! See what surprises students can create with these story starters:

- Mother reached inside the pocket and felt something move . . .
- The furry creature opened the washer lid . . .
- I forgot to take the money out of my pocket . . .
- The Timex watch was still ticking . . .
- The rinse and spin cycle was a dizzy ride for . . .

Chirp-along Math

Students chirp like crickets and listen to discover the missing math fact. Call on a child in one part of the room to chirp several times. Call on another child to chirp. Children listen and count the number of chirps, then add, subtract, or multiply the two numbers as directed. Students write the answers on their papers.

Variation: Use two metal clickers, and pass them around so everyone gets to be a cricket.

Nature Walk

Jay noticed the little things in nature, like the gray spider in a web, and his own footprints in the dust. Encourage children to look for unique things to study on a class nature walk. Without disturbing the environment, collect specimens in plastic bags for a classroom terrarium or nature table.

Vocabulary Building

The author, Rebecca Caudill, chose interesting verbs to describe the action in her story. Increase student vocabulary with these words:

whittle	climb	slither
wade	scuttle	graze
ripple	fiddle	nod
zigzag	hoot	dart

Have children use the words in sentences, add -ing, or put them in alphabetical order.

Slithering, Scuttling, Zigzagging

Ready-To-Go Pocket Pal

1. Duplicate this page.
2. Color, cut out, and paste on a 9″ × 12″ string-tie envelope. Laminate.
3. Use the pattern on page 96 to make 20 patches. Program patches with correct and incorrect math facts. Store cards in the envelope with an answer key.
4. Program additional patches with complete and incomplete sentences, long- and short-vowel words, or true and false statements. Change student directions as needed.

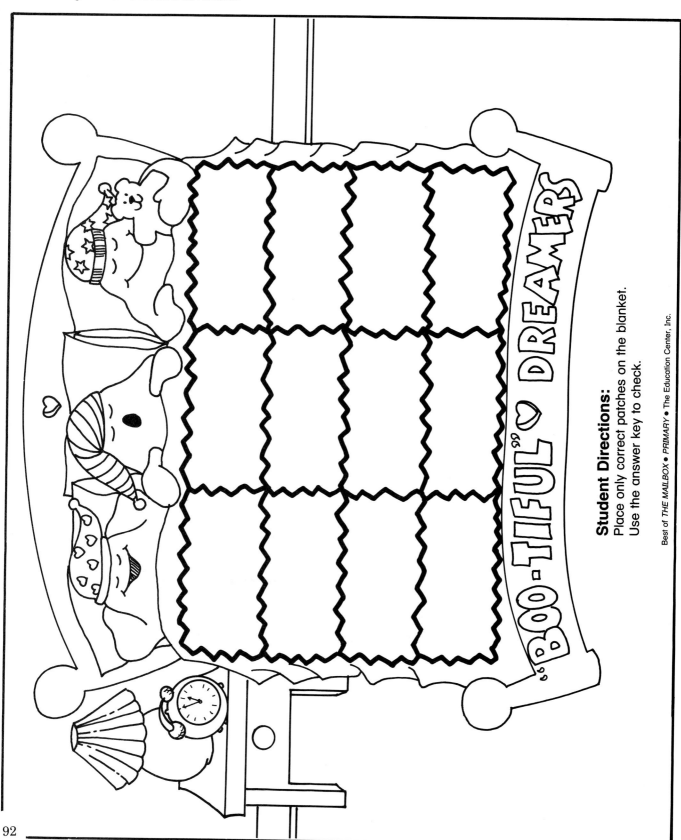

Student Directions:
Place only correct patches on the blanket.
Use the answer key to check.

Best of THE MAILBOX • PRIMARY • The Education Center, Inc.

"BOO-TIFUL DREAMERS"

Note To Teacher: Duplicate this page. Color, cut out, and mount on the front of a string-tie envelope. Laminate. Use the longhorn pattern on page 96 to make 12–15 cut-out longhorns. Label cows with correct/incorrect math facts, true/false sentences, correct/incorrect spelling words, or words with long and short vowels. Store cows in envelope with an answer key.

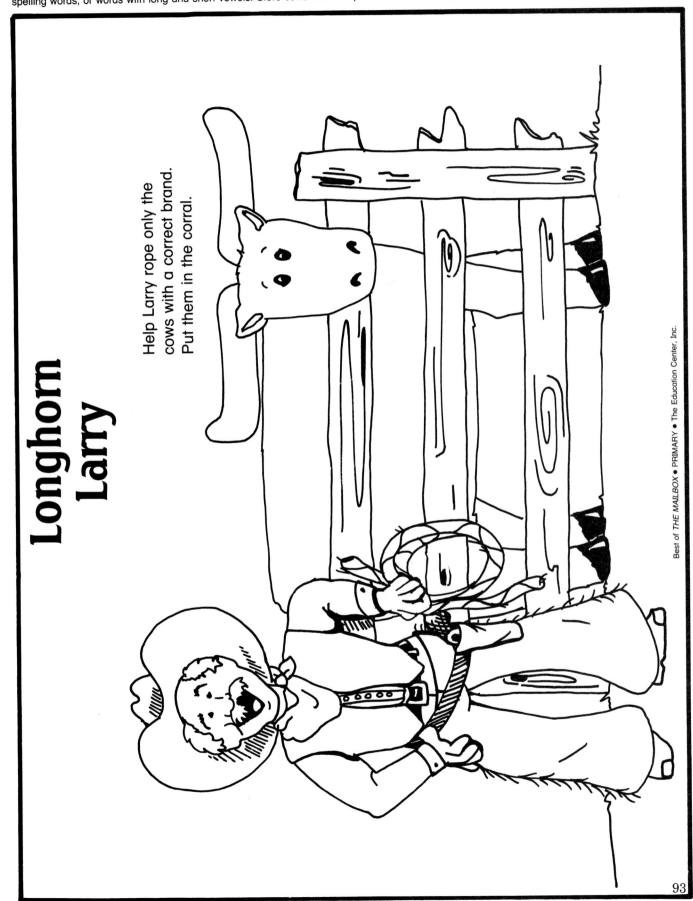

Longhorn Larry

Help Larry rope only the cows with a correct brand. Put them in the corral.

Ready-To-Go Pocket Pal

Make this cool Pocket Pal for math practice. Duplicate this page. Color, mount on a 9″ × 12″ string-tie envelope, and laminate. Make several sets of nine cards on different skills. Write corresponding answers on the envelope. Write letters to spell "let it snow" on the backs of appropriate cards, and store them in the envelope.

Let It Snow

Solve the problems on cards.
Place cards on matching ice cubes.
Turn cards over for a message.

1. Duplicate this page.
2. Color, cut out, and paste to the front of a 9" × 12" string-tie envelope.
3. Use the cupcake pattern on page 96 to make 12 tagboard cupcakes. Color and label with the months of the year. Number-code the backs of the cupcakes for self-checking. Laminate.
4. Store the cupcakes in the envelope.

Variations: Make additional sets of cupcakes to sequence letters, numbers, days of the week, story events.

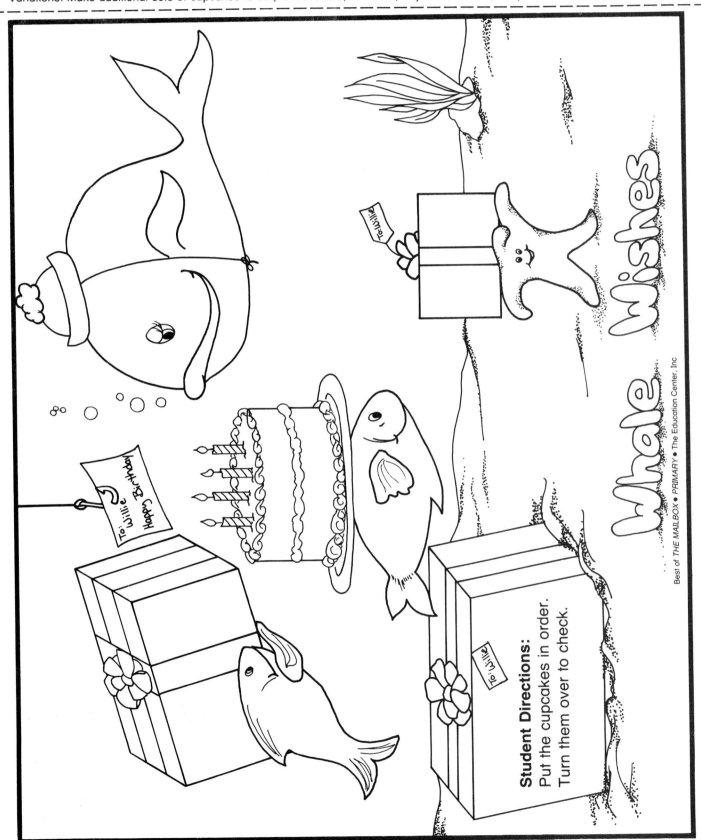

Whale Wishes

Student Directions:
Put the cupcakes in order.
Turn them over to check.

Pocket Pals Pattern Page

Use with "Longhorn Larry"
Pocket Pal on page 93.

Cupcake Pattern

Use with "Whale Wishes"
Pocket Pal on page 95.

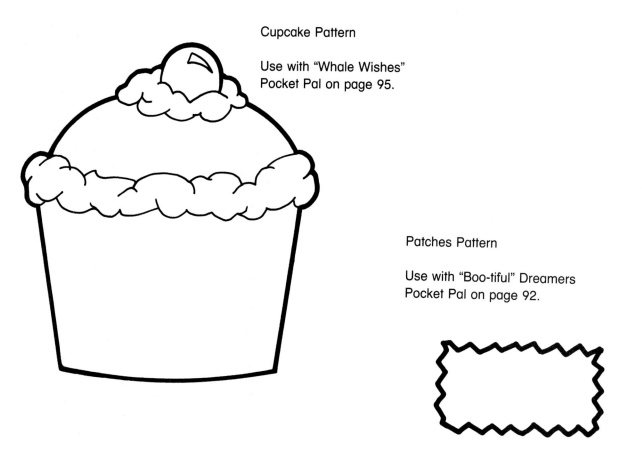

Patches Pattern

Use with "Boo-tiful" Dreamers
Pocket Pal on page 92.

Welcome to Our Pad

Join us in this chorus of spring peeper activities! See the worksheets on pages 100-102 for more croaking characters.

Take A Leap

List frog activities on lily pad cutouts and mount on a bulletin board. Display books about frogs for research and enjoyment:

Frog Goes to Dinner—M. Mayer
Frog, Where Are You?—M. Mayer
Frog Prince—E. Tarcov
Frog Went A Courtin'—J. Langstaff
Frog and Toad Together—A. Lobel

- Find out about the frog's life cycle. Draw pictures to show changes from tadpole to frog.
- Find out what a frog eats. Draw pictures of its food.
- Enjoy reading a frog book. Draw a picture of the part you liked best.
- Imagine you are a frog on a lily pad. Describe what you see.

Marie Kenzie

Frog Words And Phrases

"Rib-it" student attention on frog vocabulary. Use these for discussion starters or creative writing:

pollywogs
frog legs
spring peepers
frog kick
frogman
tadpole
garumph
croak
bullfrog
braided frogs
famous frogs—Kermit, Jeremiah

splash
ker-plop
lily pad
swamp
tree frog
bugs
amphibian
lake

What is an amphibian? Name some.

Frog Jumping Contest

Liven up flash card drill with frogs that hop along the blackboard. Back cut-out frogs and lily pads with magnetic tape. For each correct answer, teams move frog mascots closer to the finish line.

Marie Kenzie
Columbus, OH

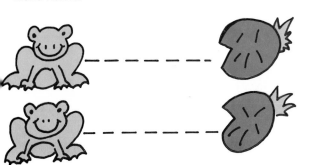

Tadpole Times

Welcome children to a pond discovery center with re-corded frog sounds, resource books, and tadpoles in an aquarium. Observe and record tadpole development. As they grow legs, substitute raw meat for their insect diet. When grown, release frog friends into the pond.

Letter From Spotty

Duplicate this letter from Swampland, and have students answer Spotty using correct letter form. Provide envelopes and place in Spotty's mailbox.

Janet Driscoll
Altamonte Springs, FL

19 Lily Pad
Swampland, FL 32000

Dear Friend,

I'm so lonesome out here in Swampland. My neighbors at 18 and 20 Lily Pad have moved. Now it's just the crickets and me watching the sun rise and set.

I was wondering if you could visit me. It would be great fun! We can swim every day. I'll teach you how to catch insects with your tongue!

Please consider my invitation and write. I hope you'll come.

Croakfully yours,
Spotty

Giant Bullfrogs

These giant bullfrogs will rivet attention in your classroom. Each child will need two paper plates, two Styrofoam cups, toothpicks, four bendable drinking straws, scissors, glue, green tempera paint, and construction paper scraps.

Directions:

1. Paint the paper plates and Styrofoam cups with green tempera paint. Cut the plates along the radius, as shown. Fold A to B, and staple. Place one cone shape on top of the other, and staple the edges together.
2. Cut the two Styrofoam cups as shown. Bottoms become eyes. Glue cut-out paper eyeballs inside the cup bottoms. Push toothpicks through the eyes, to fasten them to the top plate.
3. For legs, push straws between the bottom and the top paper plate. Insert bent straws into the remaining Styrofoam pieces for feet.
4. Glue on paper spots if desired.

Sr. Ann Claire Rhoads
Emmitsburg, MD

Lily Pad Leap

This lily pad pond will motivate students to leap to new levels of learning. Place 26 to 30 green lily pads on a bulletin board. Cut out yellow circles labeled with capital letters, lowercase letters, vocabulary words, clock faces, coin amounts, math facts, or numbers. Have each child cut out a green paper frog and move it along the path as he correctly identifies each lily pad.

Alice Frost
New Castle, DE

Put these words in alphabetical order.

frog	jump
toad	leaping
lily pad	green
amphibians	tadpoles
bullfrog	water
hop	pond
warts	insects

The ABC Frog

Skillful students will catch this frog for alphabetical order. Write the words on a laminated frog. Wipe off to add new directions and change the skill.

Kathy Graham
Twin Falls, ID

Enchanted Frog Puppet

Make a hand puppet that will enchant any child. Paint one side of a paper plate with green tempera paint. Add black dots. When dry, cover the other side of the plate with green construction paper. Cut out a large red circle, and glue to the center as shown for the tongue. Fold the plate in half.

Next make two strips of green construction paper (8" × 1"). Staple one strip to the front of the puppet, and staple one strip to the back, as shown. Be sure to leave enough space so little hands can slip through.

Cut out two eyes. Position and glue to the strip on the front. Add cut-out arms and legs. To make the frog talk, place fingers under the strips and open and close the mouth.

Kathy Graham
Twin Falls, ID

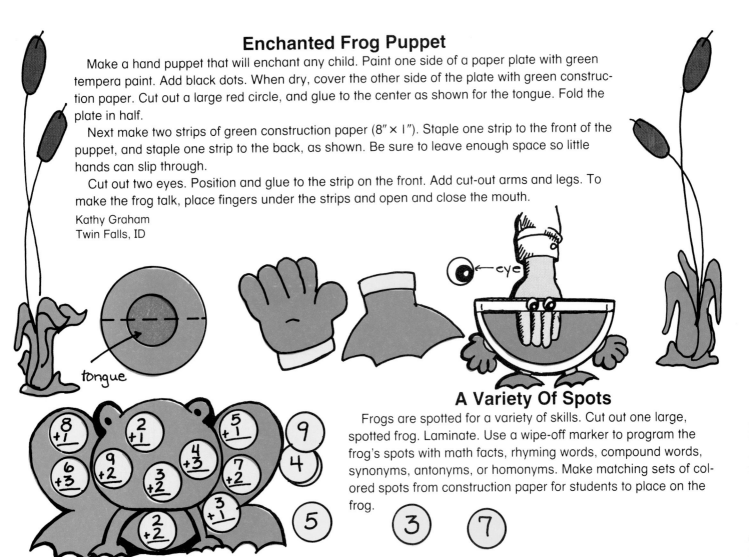

tongue

←eye

A Variety Of Spots

Frogs are spotted for a variety of skills. Cut out one large, spotted frog. Laminate. Use a wipe-off marker to program the frog's spots with math facts, rhyming words, compound words, synonyms, antonyms, or homonyms. Make matching sets of colored spots from construction paper for students to place on the frog.

Jump For Your Life

Here's how to use the reproducible on page 100 as a game for 3–4 players. Have the children make 16 butterflies from pipe cleaners and beads to use as game markers. For each butterfly marker, double a pipe cleaner, and insert it through a bead. Bend to shape four wings.

Duplicate page 100. Color and paste it on poster board. Laminate the gameboard. Make a deck of skill cards. Label the backs of cards with answers, and indicate the number of moves each corrected answer is worth.

To play, provide four butterflies for each player. Each player chooses a lily pad and places his butterflies beside it, outside the playing area. Place the skill cards faceup on the gameboard.

Student directions:

1. In turn, take the top card, read the question, and say the answer.
2. Turn it over to check. If correct, move the number of spaces it says. If incorrect, do not move.
3. If you land on another lily pad or another player's butterfly, you are caught! Place your butterfly on the frog in the center. You can start a new butterfly at any time. You can move any of your butterflies on each turn.
4. The winner is the player with the most butterflies left after all cards are drawn or when time is up.

Susan L. Nixon
Avondale, AZ

Name _____

Jump For Your Life

Note To Teacher: Program the spaces with math problems, vocabulary words, or questions. Duplicate as a worksheet for each child or as a gameboard for a group. See game directions on page 99.

Name _____

Frog And Toad

Read the information on the frog and toad.
Color the lily pads that are true.

Toads have
short legs.

Frogs have
webbed toes.

Frogs can grow
to be eight inches.

Frogs are green.

Most toads
are brown.

Toads do not
cause warts.

Bullfrogs are
not real.

There are about 250 kinds of
toads. Toads have short legs that
limit them to hopping. They do
not leap. Most toads are brown.
They do not cause warts.

Frogs have webbed toes.
Some frogs grow to a large
size. The bullfrog can grow
up to eight inches long.
Frogs are green.

Frogs are yellow.

Toads can
leap high.

Bonus Box: Write a
story about the frog and
toad who were friends.

Answer keys on pages 190 and 191.

101

Name _____

Leaping Into Long Vowels

Circle the two vowels in each word on the lily pads below.
Cut and paste each lily pad under the picture with the same vowel sound.

When two vowels go walking, the first usually does the talking.

rain   tail   coat   read   tie   bead   pie

pleat   boat   paint   goat   lie

Answer keys on pages 190 and 191.
Best of THE MAILBOX • PRIMARY • ©The Education Center, Inc. • Dona Monahan, Bristol, CT

Brush Those
Pearly Whites!

National Children's Dental Health Month is in February. In addition to a visit from the dentist, offer your students these activities to spark interest in personal dental care. Use the related worksheets on pages 104 and 105 for skills practice.

Sylvia J. Foust, Long Beach, NC

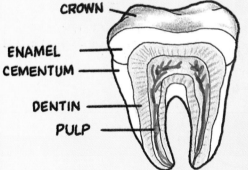

Dear Tooth Fairy, . . .

Letters to the Tooth Fairy provide a golden opportunity for creative writing and letter-writing practice. Instruct students to address envelopes to the Tooth Fairy and place them under a bed pillow on your desk. A brief hand-written response to each will add to the excitement. Older children may enjoy writing to the Tooth Fairy to convince her to raise her payments, due to the high cost of living these days. Brainstorm together what the Tooth Fairy might do with all of those teeth! (She may turn them into stars in the sky or string them on necklaces!)

Pop's Pearls

Even a hippo must eat correctly to keep nice teeth! Enlarge Pop's face on tagboard. Then cut out eight white teeth to match. Label these with healthy foods, leaving the backs blank. Label additional teeth with less healthy foods and blacken the backs. Have children place only healthy foods in Pop's mouth. When flipped over, the cards should show only pearly whites!

CROWN
ENAMEL
CEMENTUM
DENTIN
PULP

Enamel Enemies

If children have a difficult time understanding how acid works on enamel, try this experiment. Soak a raw egg in a glass of vinegar overnight. The acid will slowly soften the shell, just as acid in the mouth can cause a tooth to weaken and decay. Show a cross-sectional diagram of the inside of a tooth. The enamel is the thin outer covering that protects the tooth pulp and nerve endings inside. Discuss what happens to the inside layers when the enamel is eaten away by acid in the mouth. When the pulp is exposed, we get a tooth-ache. Ouch!

Checkup Chatter

Trips to the dentist may be scary or fun. Discuss children's fears about going to the dentist. Discuss positive feelings from a perfect checkup or a winning smile. Have children write their likes and dislikes on a large poster board tooth.

I like the prizes.
I like to see my X rays.

I don't like the smell.
I don't like the drill.

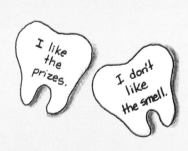

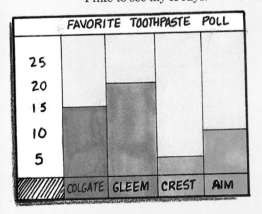

Winning Smiles

Take a favorite toothpaste poll in your classroom or school for bar-graph practice. Have students poll their classmates or other classes and record the results on a large bar-graph poster. For creative writing, ask children to write an ad for a new toothpaste that makes some outrageous claims! Design toothpaste tubes and logos for a fun bulletin board.

Tiger's New Tooth

Color the sentences that tell Tiger how to take care of his tooth.
Color Tiger.

1. Brush your teeth.

2. Eat candy bars.

3. Use dental floss.

4. Chew bubble gum.

5. Drink milk.

6. Visit the dentist.

7. Eat vegetables.

8. Rinse your mouth with water after you eat.

9. Chew ice cubes.

10. Don't snack.

Bonus Box:
Cut out Tiger.
Tape him to a straw
to make a stick
puppet.

A Gnawing Toothache

Read the paragraphs.
Cut and paste the sentences in order on another paper.

Word Box

bacteria
acid
enamel
decay
pulp

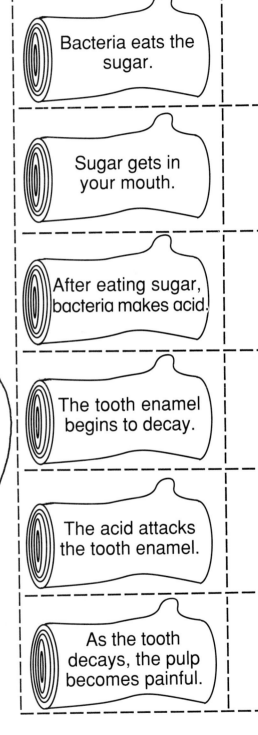

Bacteria eats the sugar.

Sugar gets in your mouth.

After eating sugar, bacteria makes acid.

The tooth enamel begins to decay.

The acid attacks the tooth enamel.

As the tooth decays, the pulp becomes painful.

There are several steps to tooth decay. When you eat a cookie, sugar gets in your mouth. A kind of bacteria in your mouth eats the sugar. This makes acid. This acid attacks the tooth enamel.

The enamel begins to decay. As the enamel decays, the acid may reach the pulp. The pulp becomes painful. You will feel a toothache.

Bonus Box: Write a story about the beaver's trip to the dentist.

Pirate Tales

Try a swashbuckling unit about pirates to encourage students to venture into language, math, and map skills. See the patterns on pages 111 and 112. Duplicate the reproducible worksheets on page 109 and 110 to provide more practice on basic skills.

Ideas by Amy Benson and Sharon Haley

X Marks The Spot

For map-reading practice, hide some pirate refreshments in several "treasure chests" on the school grounds. Have a treasure hunt! Provide maps for groups of "pirates." The first group to retrieve their treasure and return to the classroom gets a bounty of foil-wrapped chocolate "doubloons." When everyone returns, have a party to share the "booty."

Ahoy, Mateys!

Your crew will find plenty of tasks to keep them busy on this pirate ship! Enlarge the ship pattern on page 111, and mount it on a bulletin board with a list of vocabulary words. Pin task cards to the sails.

Task Cards

1. Find out what a galleon is, and draw one on a piece of paper.
2. Pretend you are a modern-day pirate. What would be in your treasure chest? Draw a picture of your treasure chest and its contents.
3. Read one of the pirate books provided. Write a book report. Tell three things you learned about pirates. Tell your favorite part of the book.
4. Pack a pirate bag! If you were a pirate going to sea, what would you pack in your suitcase? List ten things.
5. Pretend you are the captain of a pirate ship. Design your own pirate flag. Mount your flag on the bulletin board.

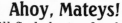

Treasure Chest

Children will discover money practice in these treasure chests. Save several small gift boxes. Have students make gold or silver foil-wrapped coins, or use play money. Children can decorate and label their "doubloons" with coin values. Place a different amount of money in each box, and write the total on the bottom. Place the treasure chests at a center. Students count out the money and check the answers.

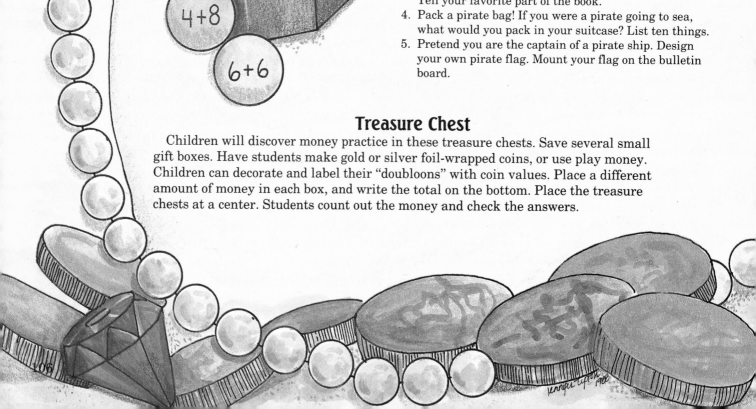

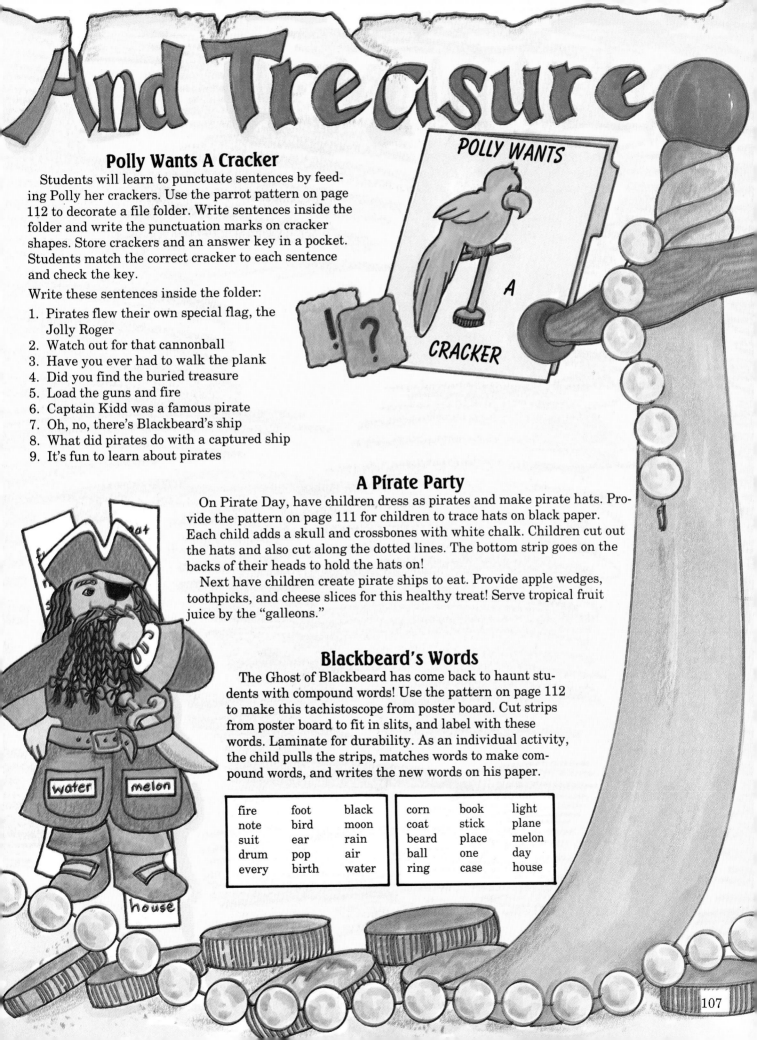

Polly Wants A Cracker

Students will learn to punctuate sentences by feeding Polly her crackers. Use the parrot pattern on page 112 to decorate a file folder. Write sentences inside the folder and write the punctuation marks on cracker shapes. Store crackers and an answer key in a pocket. Students match the correct cracker to each sentence and check the key.

Write these sentences inside the folder:

1. Pirates flew their own special flag, the Jolly Roger
2. Watch out for that cannonball
3. Have you ever had to walk the plank
4. Did you find the buried treasure
5. Load the guns and fire
6. Captain Kidd was a famous pirate
7. Oh, no, there's Blackbeard's ship
8. What did pirates do with a captured ship
9. It's fun to learn about pirates

A Pirate Party

On Pirate Day, have children dress as pirates and make pirate hats. Provide the pattern on page 111 for children to trace hats on black paper. Each child adds a skull and crossbones with white chalk. Children cut out the hats and also cut along the dotted lines. The bottom strip goes on the backs of their heads to hold the hats on!

Next have children create pirate ships to eat. Provide apple wedges, toothpicks, and cheese slices for this healthy treat! Serve tropical fruit juice by the "galleons."

Blackbeard's Words

The Ghost of Blackbeard has come back to haunt students with compound words! Use the pattern on page 112 to make this tachistoscope from poster board. Cut strips from poster board to fit in slits, and label with these words. Laminate for durability. As an individual activity, the child pulls the strips, matches words to make compound words, and writes the new words on his paper.

fire	foot	black	corn	book	light
note	bird	moon	coat	stick	plane
suit	ear	rain	beard	place	melon
drum	pop	air	ball	one	day
every	birth	water	ring	case	house

Treasure Maps

Your students will enjoy making their own treasure maps. Have each child bring in a brown grocery bag and tear it apart. Crinkle up a piece of bag, about 8" × 10" in size, and wet it under the faucet. Children use their hands to smooth out the papers. While the paper is still wet, have each student draw a map with chalk. Let the maps dry. The end result is an authentic-looking treasure map.

Display the maps, and encourage children to write stories about their maps. Ask these questions: What is in the treasure chest? Where did it come from? Who else knows about it? How did it get buried?

First Mate's Game

Here's a game for two to eight players in which your "crew" members can show their skill at the wheel! Enlarge the ship's wheel on page 111 on poster board. Color and laminate the gameboard. Provide a spinner and game markers. Write vocabulary words, math problems, or questions on the playing board. Each player chooses a spoke of the wheel. He must follow this path to reach the center. To play, children spin and move their markers in turn. Each child answers the question he lands on. If correct, he stays. If incorrect, he goes back. The first player to reach the center becomes the First Mate and wins!

Yo, Ho, Ho! Pirate Puppets!

Send up the Jolly Roger! Invite the class to step back into the times when buccaneers roamed the open seas. Set the stage for a pirate puppet show by reading excerpts from *Treasure Island*. To make pirate puppets, have students bring in old socks. Stuff socks with old nylon stockings, and add features, earrings, and pieces of cloth. Name the puppets, and create a script with this motley crew of characters. Set the scene on a treasure ship, and make the villains walk the plank!

Math Treasure Hunt

Students will find a gold mine of math practice on this treasure hunt! Spray paint some rocks with gold paint. Write a math equation on each one with a marker. Hide the rocks in the classroom or on the school grounds. Duplicate the worksheet on page 110, and pass out these answer sheets. Each pirate must find a gold rock, write the answer on his treasure chest, and replace the rock for the next pirate to find.

Give the class a time limit and these rules: Pirates must walk. Pirates are quiet. Pirates sit down when they have found all of their gold! Pirates with perfect scores get a reward.

Blackbeard's Secret

Circle the letter in the fact or the opinion column.
Write the letters in the numbered blanks below to solve the mystery.

	Fact	Opinion
1. The word "pirate" means sea robber.	A	Y
2. The Age of Pirates was over 200 years ago.	E	F
3. All pirates were ugly.	G	T
4. Pirates were outlaws.	D	O
5. The pirates voted for their captain.	W	B
6. Pirates had rules to share the treasure.	C	K
7. Captain Kidd was the most dangerous pirate.	Q	R
8. Some pirates were women.	H	S
9. Black Bart was meaner than Calico Jack.	I	E
10. Walking the plank was better than hanging.	M	A
11. Today, air pirates are called hijackers.	D	P

What was Blackbeard's real name?

___ ___ ___ ___ ___ ___   ___ ___ ___ ___ ___
 2   4   5   1   7   11   3   9   10   6   8

Gold From The Spanish Main

1. _____   6. _____   11. _____

2. _____   7. _____   12. _____

3. _____   8. _____   13. _____

4. _____   9. _____   14. _____

5. _____   10. _____   15. _____

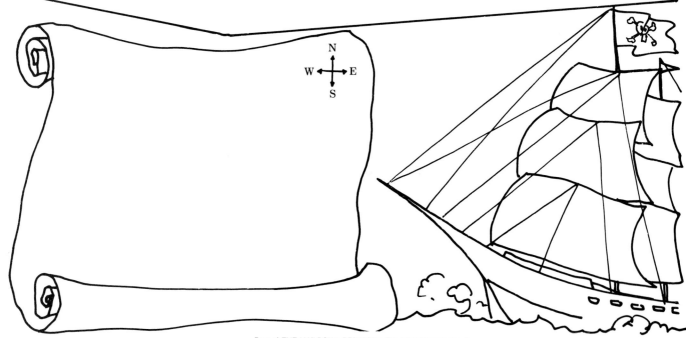

Note To Teacher: Use this for "Math Treasure Hunt" on page 108.

Pirate Patterns

Enlarge for the bulletin board idea, "Ahoy, Mateys," on page 106.

Enlarge to trace pirate hats for "A Pirate Party" on page 107.

Enlarge for "First Mate's Game" on page 108.

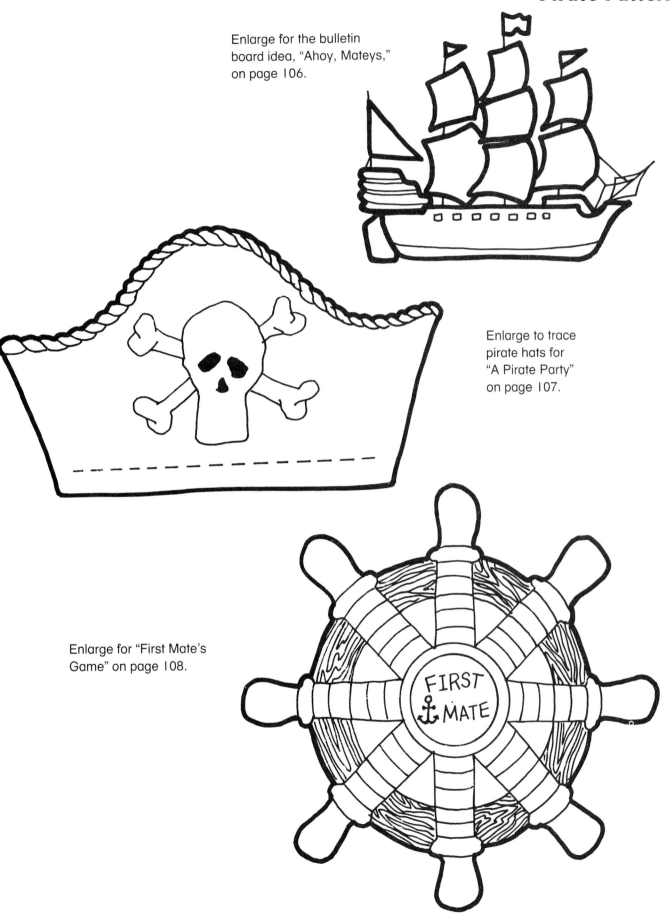

FIRST MATE

Pirate Patterns

Use with "Polly Wants a Cracker" on page 107.

Use for "Blackbeard's Words" on page 107.

JELLY BEANS

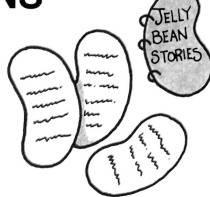

The Tale Of A Jelly Bean

Encourage creative writing with jelly bean-shaped story starter cards. Have students write jelly bean stories on any of these topics:

The World's Biggest Jelly Bean
The Day It Rained Jelly Beans
The Jelly Bean Quarry

The Day the Jelly Bean Lost Its Color
The Bird That Laid Jelly Beans
The Adventures of Jeremy Jelly Bean

Put all the stories together in a class book with a colorful jelly bean cover.

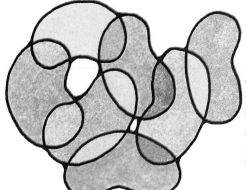

Jumbled Jelly Beans

Bean shapes turn to jelly in colorful, jumbled designs. Have children overlap and trace a jelly bean pattern over and over on their papers. Each student then colors all overlapping areas in one color and adds contrasting colors to the remaining areas. Vary this idea with personal patterns and monochromatic color schemes.

Pamela M. Hartley
Twin Falls, ID

Spill The Beans

Cut out ten colorful, jelly bean-shaped pieces. Store them with directions in a Styrofoam cup. Have students "spill" the beans onto the table and follow the directions on their own papers. Program cutouts with scrambled spelling words, mixed-up sentences to put in correct order, sentences to punctuate, or events to sequence.

Mary Anne T. Haffner
Waynesboro, PA

Directions: Unscramble the word on each jelly bean.

My Own Jar Of Jelly Beans

Duplicate a copy of this jelly bean jar on oaktag for each child. Each time a child reads a book, he colors in a jelly bean. Longer books merit two jelly beans. Display jars to see who has read the most.

Susan Child
Front Royal, VA

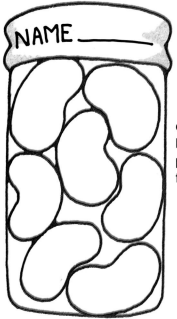

NAME _____

Sweet Charts And Graphs

Provide several bags of jelly beans for lots of charting practice. Divide students into groups, and give each group a bag. Children spread the candies out on a desk. They separate them by color, then tally the number of each color. Have each group choose a line, circle, bar, or pictograph style and create one to show the number of candies of each color. You may want to provide skeleton formats of each style of graph.

BAR GRAPH
Orange
Yellow
Pink
Black

PICTOGRAPH
White   o o o
Green   o o o o
Red   o o
Pink   o o o

CIRCLE GRAPH
RED
ORANGE
PINK
GREEN

LINE GRAPH
5 4 3 2 1
RED YELLOW ORANGE PINK

Today's Flavors

Vanilla
Cherry
Mint Chocolate Chip
Orange Swirl
Chocolate
Strawberry
Almond Nut

"I scream, you scream, we all scream for ice cream." Reading, writing, and 'rithmetic will all be reinforced through the wide choice of flavorful activities. Add the worksheet on page 116 for more fun.

Banana Splits Reading Clubs

These banana splits are concocted by reading books. Club guidelines should be established and posted with the display:

Club Requirements

1. Banana	Read 4 books.
2. Spoon	Read 5 books.
3. Ice Cream	Read 5 books. Report on one.
4. Chocolate	Read 6 books, including: (choose from a list)
5. Whipped Cream	Read 6 books. Make a book jacket or poster for one.
6. Cherry	Read 7 books. Make a diorama for one.

Students may join only one club each week. They fill their dishes as they join.

Follow up with a banana split party.

Jenan Merrill
Columbia, TN

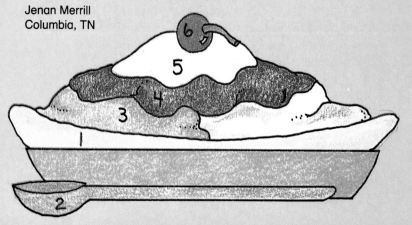

Cool Contractions

Students who can match these Popsicles and sticks are licking contractions. Cut out and laminate Popsicles, and label with contractions. Mark Popsicle sticks with words forming the contraction. Students match, write answers, and use each contraction in a sentence.

Trish Frazier
Broken Bow, OK

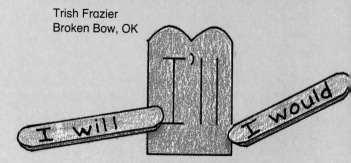

Favorite Flavors

Alphabetize the following list of frozen treat flavors:

caramel	orange sherbet
strawberry	chocolate
chocolate chip	banana
maple nut	peach
vanilla	butter pecan
butter brickle	lime sherbet
cherry nut	rocky road

Judy Sill
Loveland, CO

Ice Cream

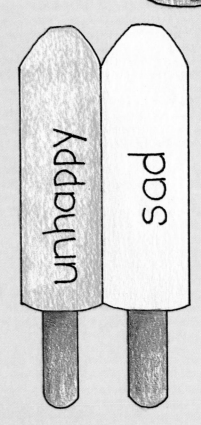

Class Favorites

Students can practice graph-making skills with a class picture graph. Each child adds and colors a cone showing his favorite flavor. Follow up with questions to analyze the results (most popular, average, least popular).

Extension: Use different chart or graph styles for this topic (line, circle, bar, tally).

Barbara Stringer
Loveland, OH

Popsicle Twins

No Popsicle is complete with only one half. Cut out and laminate Popsicles. Cut in half, and label with one of a pair of synonyms. Students match, write, and check.

Trish Frazier

Stack A Cone

Triple scoops are the goal of this matching exercise. Cut out and laminate cones and three colorful scoops for each one. Program cones with numbers and scoops with the number word, set, and dot pattern. Students match, write answers, and check.

Variation: Program these for multiple meanings of words, months in a season, or the four food groups.

Lucille Miller
Sacramento, CA

Name _____

Soft Serve With A Twist

Note To Teacher: Use for creative writing, spelling tests, or assignments.

Corny Popcorn Capers

Create a popcorn explosion in your classroom with creative movement, reading, cooking, and art ideas.

Popcorn Trivia
- Popcorn only has 25 to 55 calories per cup without butter.
- Each American eats an average of 2½ pounds of popcorn annually.
- Fossil drawings in caves indicate popcorn has been around since 2500 BC.
- Pilgrims ate popcorn as a breakfast food. A complete breakfast might have included milk, popcorn, berries, and honey or brown sugar.
- Quadequina was the Indian who brought popcorn to the first Thanksgiving feast.

How Was Popcorn Discovered?

Read *The Popcorn Dragon* by Jane Thayer to the class. Challenge your students to imagine how popcorn might have first been discovered. Cut writing paper into popcorn shapes and ask students to write their ideas. Display the popcorn compositions on a bulletin board.

"Pop" Art

Long ago, Mexican Indians preferred to make jewelry out of popcorn rather than eat it. Students will love an opportunity to create necklaces or bracelets from popcorn as the Indians did. Provide students with dull-pointed needles and dental floss. Have children string their own jewelry using popcorn, raisins, jelly beans, and gumdrops. The children will enjoy modeling their original jewelry fashions at lunch one day.

Children will be popping up with correct answers when you challenge them to a game of "Popcorn." Prepare flash cards in advance for the appropriate skill or skills to be drilled. Stand at the front of the room so that the cards can be seen by everyone. To begin play, one student will stand beside another student. Only these two students will compete for the first answer. Flash the drill card. The first student to call out the correct answer will "pop" to the next desk to compete against the next student. The student left behind takes a seat in the empty desk or remains seated. Play continues in this manner. At the conclusion of the game, remember to compliment those students who were very quick and accurate.

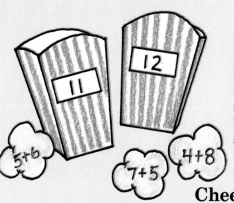

Popcorn Classification

Create a center that looks good enough to eat! You will need several popcorn boxes. Label popcorn cut-outs with math facts. The student will drop each piece into the appropriate popcorn box. To make this center self-checking, glue a key to the back of each box. Vary this center by labeling popcorn with pictures to be sorted by initial sounds.

Cheesy Popcorn Snack

Improve the flavor of your measurement and fractions review with a cooking experience. Post the recipe and have students prepare their own cheese popcorn. Remember to schedule this event with your cafeteria manager ahead of time.

    2 quarts popped popcorn
    ¾ cup grated cheese (cheddar, parmesan)
    ½ teaspoon salt
    ½ cup butter

Spread popped popcorn in a shallow pan that has been buttered. Melt butter. Add grated cheese and salt to butter. Pour this mixture over the popcorn. Bake at 275 degrees for five to ten minutes or until cheese melts. Cool and serve.

Let's Get Poppin'

Youngsters will enjoy sequencing practice in this "string-along" center. Collect popcorn boxes. On white or yellow construction paper, duplicate a popcorn pattern. Laminate and punch holes as indicated. Label popcorn with words to alphabetize, sentences to be put in the correct order, months to put in order, or any other sequential practice task. Since you'll want several sets of these, color-code each set. Complete the color coding by dropping in a piece of matching yarn. Program the backs of pieces for self-checking if desired. The student will select a box of popcorn and "string" it in the correct order.

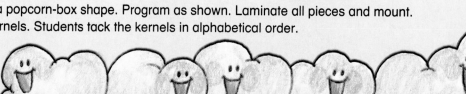

Popcorn Unlimited

Make 16 construction paper popcorn kernels. On each kernel, write one of the following gourmet flavors:

bacon	cherry	nacho cheese	raspberry
butter	grape	orange	sour cream and onion
caramel	honey	pizza	taco
cheese	mint	plain	watermelon

Use tagboard to make a popcorn-box shape. Program as shown. Laminate all pieces and mount. Use pushpins to mount kernels. Students tack the kernels in alphabetical order.

Paula Holdren
Prospect, KY

Popcorn Punctuation

Read the story. Glue kernels of popcorn where periods are needed.
Then cut out the capital letter kernels and glue them where capital letters
should be.

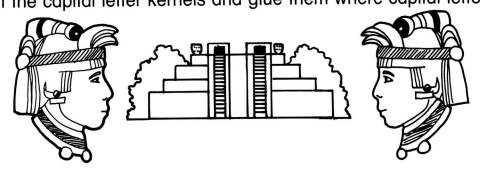

long, long ago, Indians thought there were spirits in

popcorn   they   believed   that   corn   popped   when

the   spirits   broke   out   of   the   kernel

today   we   know   that   there   are   no   spirits   in

popcorn   when   popcorn   is   heated,   steam   is   made

in   the   kernel   as   the   corn   gets   hotter,

the   steam   presses   harder   and   harder   on   the   kernel

at   last   the   steam   makes   the   popcorn   pop   open

Bonus Box: Draw a picture that shows what Indians believed made popcorn pop. Then draw a picture that shows what really makes popcorn pop.

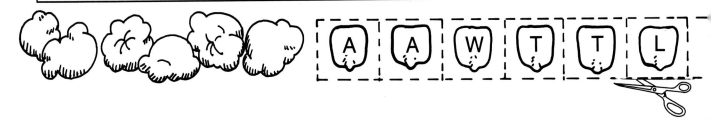

Note to teacher: Duplicate this page on multicolored construction paper. Provided popped popcorn without butter. Have students read and follow directions.

Best of THE MAILBOX • PRIMARY • The Education Center, Inc.   Answer keys on pages 190 and 191.   119

PIZZA!

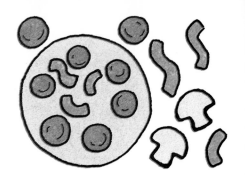

Pizza is to eat! You bet it is, but look what else you can do. My first-grade class loved using pizza as the motivational tool for activities that touched many curriculum areas. Celebrate Pizza Month in October with these mouth-watering activities!

Paper Pizza Collage

Yum-yum! Students can picture a delicious pizza! Provide orange and yellow shredded tissue paper and multicolored construction paper for students to cut any ingredients they desire. Stack and paste tempting combinations. Display or use as covers for books of class pizza activities.

A Slice Of Pizza Pie

Matching pieces create a whole pizza pie. Write items that match on sections of construction paper circles. Cut wedges apart, and mix pieces from several pies. Students assemble. Program with synonyms, math facts, or number activities.

Pizza Assembly Line Bake Off

Bake minipizzas to motivate children to sequence, follow directions, identify four food groups, and cooperate.

Materials for each student:
1 refrigerator biscuit
1 tbsp. spaghetti sauce
flour
1 large pinch grated cheese
chopped olives
parsley flakes

Roll biscuit out flat on floured surface. Spoon on and spread sauce. Sprinkle on cheese. Top with olives and parsley flakes. Transfer to cookie sheet. Bake at 450 degrees for 12 minutes. Enjoy!

Pizzeria Pizzazz

Whet appetites for pizza by decorating the room with menus, picture advertisements, coupons, napkins, and place mats from pizza eateries. Then use these for activities such as marking words that begin with *p* or have a certain vowel sound, counting and alphabetizing ingredients, or marking most/least expensive items on a menu.

Pinch A Pizza Wheel

Many pizza parlors donate cardboard wheels for classroom use. Program pizza wheels and clip clothespins with math facts and answers, pictures and beginning consonants, clock faces and times. Add answers on the back of the wheel. If you use colored plastic clothespins, students can clip by color. (Example: ō = orange, ā = yellow, ī = brown).

Spin A Pizza

Students try their hand at twirling these pizzas for practice. Cut pairs of oaktag circles. Laminate and cut a wedge from one circle in each pair. Fasten pairs with a brad in the center. Spin to program with skill work, pizza story starters, or ingredients for pizzas. Decorate as desired. Vary as students spin out "pizza-rific" work!

cheese	ll
sausage	l
bacon	l
pepperoni	llll
hamburger	l

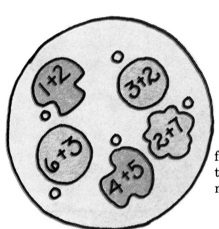

My Favorite Pizza

A cardboard pizza wheel makes a great chart. Students sign up for their favorite and discuss results. We shared the chart with our principal who treated us to our favorite pizza, pepperoni! We wrote him a great thank-you note on—what else? A large paper pizza!

Pizza Poke And Peek

Students poke a straw through this pizza for skill review. Program oaktag pizzas with math facts or words missing letters. Draw ingredients around problems, laminate, and use a paper drill to punch a hole near each problem. Add answers on the back. Provide a straw for poke-and-peek fun!

Pizza To Go

Wrap up pizza fun by combining materials from the unit (including the recipe) into a stapled book to take home. Top it with the collage.

An Apple For The Teacher

Stuffed Apples

Hang stuffed apples from branches for an activity tree or mobile. Stuff two stapled, tissue paper apple shapes with cotton balls or more tissue. Add a twist of green tissue for a stem, and attach green yarn to hang. Display apples with tasks to complete on a branch set in sand or hang as a mobile.

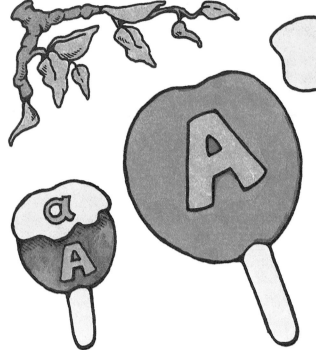

Caramel Apples

Caramel apples are a treat for skills practice. Cut out red construction paper apples and brown caramel toppings. Glue a Popsicle stick to the back of each apple. Children match the caramel topping to the apple for upper-/lowercase letter matching, beginning sounds, or math facts.

Ella Gainer
Mount Joy, PA

Apple Picking Time

Pick these apples for practice with synonyms, antonyms, or homonyms. Cut out apple shapes, laminate, and cut slits. Use a wipe-off crayon to label apples with words below slits. Label cut-out worms with matching words. Children slide worms into slits to match. Vary by changing the skill on apples and worms.

Clara Presutti
Bridgeport, OH

WORM PATTERN

Apple Pie Incentive

Students "bake" their apple pies by adding pieces earned for improved behavior or good work. Make one construction paper pie for each student and cut each into equal pieces. Organize a "bake-off" for students who complete their pies. Slice apples, sprinkle with sugar and cinnamon, and bake in a prepared crust. Share with everyone to celebrate!

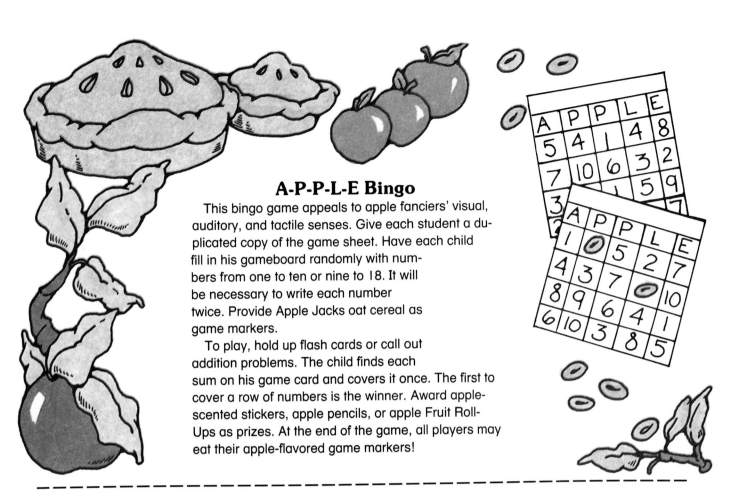

A-P-P-L-E Bingo

This bingo game appeals to apple fanciers' visual, auditory, and tactile senses. Give each student a duplicated copy of the game sheet. Have each child fill in his gameboard randomly with numbers from one to ten or nine to 18. It will be necessary to write each number twice. Provide Apple Jacks oat cereal as game markers.

To play, hold up flash cards or call out addition problems. The child finds each sum on his game card and covers it once. The first to cover a row of numbers is the winner. Award apple-scented stickers, apple pencils, or apple Fruit Roll-Ups as prizes. At the end of the game, all players may eat their apple-flavored game markers!

Name _____ Addition facts

🍎🍎🍎🍎🍎🍎🍎 Apple Bingo 🍎🍎🍎🍎🍎🍎🍎

A	P	P	L	E

STRAWBERRY PATCH

Strawberry Suckers

Glue laminated strawberry shapes to green Popsicle sticks for a taste of math practice. Write problems on strawberries and answers on the backs of the sticks. Reprogram suckers with compound words, antonyms, synonyms, or homonyms.

Jeanette Fields
Merna, NE

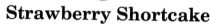

Strawberry Shortcake

Cut ten individual shortcakes from tagboard. Cut out many strawberries. On each shortcake, print a number word from one to ten. Children place the correct number of berries on each cake.

Judy Lee
Letcher, SD

Strawberry Sensations

Have a sensational Strawberry Day in your classroom! Children use their five senses with these activities:
- Make strawberry jam, Jell-O, shortcake, or candy for a treat.
- Visit a strawberry farm. Pick a pint and a quart of berries. Compare number of berries in each measure.
- Play a circle listening game. When children hear a berry word other than strawberry, they run "home." Examples: raspberries, huckleberries, blackberries, gooseberries, blueberries, cranberries, boysenberries, mulberries.
- Make strawberry-scented candles.
- Form salt and flour dough strawberries on toothpicks. When dry paint red, and add black dots with marker. Insert berries into a clay or Styrofoam block in a berry basket.

Label berries on these runners with numbers. Have students count by fives to fill in the missing berries.

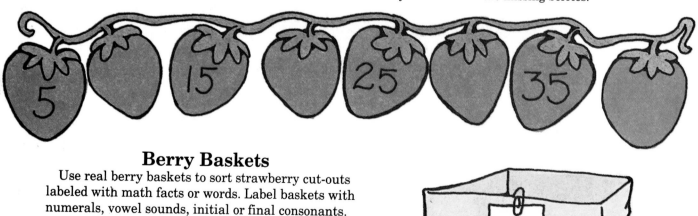

Berry Baskets

Use real berry baskets to sort strawberry cut-outs labeled with math facts or words. Label baskets with numerals, vowel sounds, initial or final consonants.

Strawberry Tasks

1. Count the "berries" in the jar. (Use red ball fringe.)
2. Make a "berry" nice card for a friend.
3. Write a strawberry story using these words:
   berry, red, huge, ate, stomachache.
4. How many words can you find in strawberry?
   Make a list.
5. Put strawberry words in ABC order.
6. Illustrate uses for luscious strawberries.

TASK CARD
PATTERN

Place these strawberry task cards in a basket. Students choose an activity and color in a strawberry on their record sheets when finished.

Each day in May, pick the strawberry labeled with the date from the basket and add it to the blank calendar.

More "Berry" Nice Ideas

- Dip strawberries in melted chocolate and eat! Listen to the indescribably delicious comments.
- Grow a strawberry plant.
- Make compound words by pairing words written on strawberry cutouts.
- Have students list *str-* cluster words.
- Make a strawberry cookbook. Children bring in their favorite strawberry recipes.

125

Christmas Around The World

Planning a classroom holiday party? Instead of the usual classroom Christmas party, include a few customs from different lands in your festivities. Decorate a class tree with ornaments representing different countries. Your students will be celebrating *and* learning about different cultures!

 In Mexico, children celebrate by breaking a suspended *piñata*. Set aside several class sessions for children to make a papier-mâché piñata. Fill it with individual sandwich bags filled with wrapped candies, sugarless gum, and balloons. Position children at a safe distance from the child swinging the stick. When the piñata is broken, each child retrieves one bag of goodies.

 In Africa, Christmas festivities include native African dances around bonfires. In South Africa, there are parades and fireworks. Africans of European descent celebrate Christmas as their English, French, and Dutch relatives do. In Ghana, Father Christmas comes from the jungles rather than the North Pole. Together, create a story about "Santa on Safari."

In France, children place their shoes by the fireplace for *Père Nöel* to fill with gifts on December 24. Play a relay game in which each child runs to a line, removes his shoes, and runs back to tag the next player on his team. Have an older child dressed as Father Christmas put wrapped treats in all of the empty shoes when the relay is over.

 In England, Father Christmas brings gifts to children. Other gifts are given on Boxing Day, December 26. On Christmas Eve, carolers gather in town squares. Provide the words for students to sing along to recorded Christmas carols. Offer a taste of fruitcake or plum pudding to classroom carolers.

In Japan and China, pine trees are decorated with red paper lanterns, paper fans, and wind chimes. On Christmas Eve in China, there is a lantern parade. Make red, paper lanterns or paper fans for the classroom tree.

 In Denmark, the national colors are red and white. Christmas trees are decorated with red-and-white paper chains and heart-shaped, woven baskets. Make a long, red-and-white paper chain for the class tree.

 In India, Christians decorate banana or coconut trees. Serve banana slices dipped in chocolate syrup and rolled in coconut.

 In Sweden, ginger cookies are hung on small wooden trees called *pepparkakor trees*. Evergreen trees are decorated with stars, sunbursts, and snowflakes made from straw. Other decorations include colorful wooden animals and straw centerpieces. Make Swedish centerpieces by tying bundles of straw together with red ribbon. Children add miniature blue-and-yellow Swedish flags made from paper.

 In Germany, children hang decorated gingerbread cookies, or *lebkuchens*, on their Christmas trees. Help children make gingerbread cookies to decorate and hang on a tree. Make some extras to eat at the party!

 In Canada, French-speaking families end the holiday season with a feast on January 6. A special fruitcake is baked with a bean and pea in it. The boy and girl who find these surprises in their pieces of cake are named the King and Queen of the Twelfth Night. Serve cupcakes with a dried bean baked in one and a pea in another. Crown the girl and boy who find the hidden prizes. Give the King and Queen for the Day special privileges.

In Spain, Puerto Rico, Mexico, and throughout Central and South America, families display manger scenes called *nacimientos*. The figure of the baby Jesus is not added until Christmas Eve. The Three Kings are said to bring gifts to children on January 6. The children leave their shoes filled with carrots, barley, or straw for the camels of the Three Kings. Play a party game in which each team passes a carrot along a line of children. The first team to "feed the camel" at the end of the line wins!

In Italy, gifts are brought by *Gesù-Bambino*, not Santa Claus. Children write notes to their parents promising to be good. The notes are hidden in the father's napkin or under his plate. After the meal, he reads them aloud. Surprise students with little notes or awards tucked into their Christmas party napkins. Have children write and decorate notes for their parents.

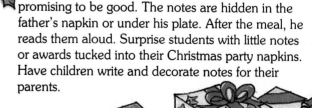

Dozens of Doughnuts

Delight your students with a fun-filled batch of doughnutty learning activities. Use the "Doughnut Dunkers" Pocket Pal on page 129 and the worksheet on page 128 to extend this unit with a variety of doughnut skills.

Doughnut Disasters

Read Robert McCloskey's *Homer Price* about the incredible doughnut machine. Have children create their own doughnut disasters and write newspaper accounts or illustrate them. Here are some possible headlines:

Coffee and Doughnuts Cause Chaos
Doughnut Holes Missing
Dollars for Doughnuts
Slam Dunkin' Doughnuts
A Hole in One
Dangerous Doughnuts
Doughnuts Discovered in Bed
Flying Doughnuts Visit Earth

Soggy Doughnuts

Try this game for some "holesome" recreation. Divide the class into teams. Have team members stand behind a line and throw wet sponge doughnut shapes into a wading pool or bucket. Teams score a point for each dunked doughnut while they cool off on hot days on the playground!

Disappearing Doughnuts

Classroom doughnuts disappear for management or student motivation. Tack up a paper doughnut for each child. To reward a student for a perfect paper, completed homework assignment, or good behavior, take a "bite" out of his doughnut by tearing a piece off. After a given number of bites, the student earns a real doughnut treat. Children see their progress as doughnuts dwindle.

Dialing For Doughnuts

Students read a batch of books and write their favorite titles on doughnut cut-outs for a bulletin board. Enlarge the pattern below, and mount on a bulletin board. Add title and student doughnuts.

Missing Doughnut Holes

Holes are needed to put these doughnuts in alphabetical order. Cut and label about 20 doughnuts and holes with letters of the alphabet. Children fill each doughnut with the missing letter. Store pieces in a "Munchkins" doughnut hole box. Make more doughnuts and holes to sequence numbers and days of the week.

Bonnie Pinkerton
Bowling Green, KY

Name _____

Making "Hole" Sentences

Cut and paste the correct hole on each doughnut.

Bill ate —— orange.

She read —— book.

She gave the teacher —— hug.

I want —— ice cream cone.

Is that —— animal?

The chicken laid —— egg.

This is —— easy job.

He asked —— question.

an

an

an

an

a

an

an

a

a

Best of *THE MAILBOX* • *PRIMARY* • The Education Center, Inc. • Sandra Nolte Schaack, Forest, VA   Answer keys on pages 190 and 191.

1. Color a photocopy of this page. Cut on the bold lines.
2. Paste the Pocket Pal on a 9" × 12" string-tie envelope.
3. Make doughnut-shaped question cards programmed for any skill. Store in the envelope with an answer key, a coin, and game pawns.

Student directions:
1. In turn, flip a coin. Heads—Move 2 spaces. Tails—Move 1 space.
2. Draw a doughnut card. Give the answer. Check the answer key.
3. If correct, stay. If incorrect, go back to your original space.
4. First to reach FINISH is a Doughnut Dunker!

Doughnut Dunkers

FINISH

START

129

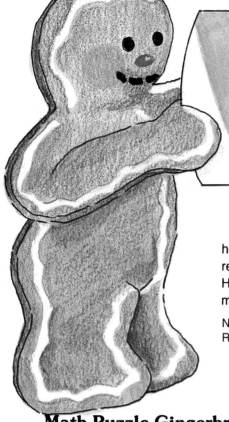

Gingerbread

Gingerbread Center

Set up a gingerbread center this holiday season! Cut out pictures of gingerbread houses and cookies from magazines and use as a background. Post a gingerbread recipe at the center and put ingredients on flash cards for children to alphabetize. Have children sequence paper strips with recipe steps written on them. Finally, make gingerbread for the whole class to eat!

Nancy McDivett
Reading, PA

Math Puzzle Gingerbread House

This gingerbread house can be assembled by children who know their math facts. Cut out a house shape and divide it into puzzle pieces. Label each puzzle piece with a math problem that equals the number on the roof. Decorate and cut apart the puzzle. Give children several puzzle houses to sort through and put together under the correct roofs.

Connie Harper
Parishville, NY

Gingerbread Cookie Cutouts

Make lots of gingerbread cookie cutouts by tracing around a cookie cutter. Try some of these "recipes" for fun!

- Give each child a gingerbread man and have him build a scene around it.

- Make stuffed gingerbread men. Trace two identical shapes on 9" × 12" construction paper. Cut out, decorate, stuff, and staple. Make smaller men for tree ornaments.

- Use wallpaper or gift wrap, and have each child decorate his gingerbread man in clothing.

- Label cutouts with words to put in alphabetical order or with numbers to sequence.

- Place cookie combinations on a cookie sheet for addition and subtraction practice.

Nancy McDivett

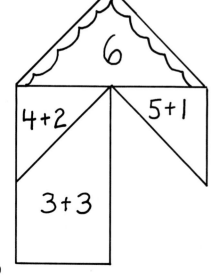

Time

The Cookie Sheet Matchup

Use this gingerbread "cookie sheet" for a small group math game. Each child gets one duplicated sheet of cookie answers. Children, in turn, take construction paper cookies labeled with math problems from a cookie jar and match them with the correct answers on their cookie sheets. The first one to cover his cookie sheet wins!

Mary Jo Morrisey
Batavia, NY

Cookie Pan Learning Center

Use an old cookie sheet covered with Con-Tact paper for a two-sided center. Magnetic tape holds the activity pieces on the pan.

Glenda Robinson
Augusta, GA

magnetic tape

Con-Tact paper

The Gingerbread Bakery

Children can bake up some gingerbread words by putting them in a bulletin board oven. Make two ovens and post a sign for nouns or verbs on each oven door. Cut out cookie shapes from construction paper. Label with vocabulary words. Children take a cookie shape from the bowl and place it in the correct oven.

The Gingerbread Cookie Race

This game for two players is a fun way to practice sequencing. Make two identical sets of gingerbread cutouts from brown and tan poster board. Label with numbers. Give each player one set of cookies. At a signal, players race to see who can put his cards in order first.

Marilyn Hall
Clemons, IA

A gingerbread cookie pattern is provided on page 23.

A Rainbow of

Explore the world of color with your class by using this colorful spectrum of activities.

Mixing Colors

Children can experience the excitement of making secondary colors from primary red, yellow, and blue with these activities:

- Provide two primary colors of finger paint or tempera for children to mix to discover the secondary color created.
- Have students make two watercolor washes on a sheet of white paper.
- Tear tissue paper of primary colors into pieces, and have children make "stained glass" colors on the windows.
- Cut out shapes of cellophane or colored plastic, and place on an overhead projector as overlays.
- Mix colored water in a glass dish placed on an overhead projector. Project the new colors on the screen as you mix tints.

Colorburst

Children will be surprised by a color explosion if they follow these directions:

- Fill an aluminum pie tin about ½ full of milk.
- Add a few drops of red, green, blue, and yellow food coloring around the edges. (Do not stir!)
- Add some liquid soap, a drop or two at a time, and observe.

The colorburst will delight the children, and cleanup will be easy.

Color Experiment

This experiment with mixing colors will produce unique results you will want to frame and display. Provide these materials at a center: white dinner napkins; red, yellow, and blue food coloring in cups of water; and plastic eyedroppers.

Directions: Have one child at a time experiment with the color solutions by dropping colored water drops on a folded white dinner napkin. Do not open napkins until dry to prevent tearing. Place between folded construction paper to frame.

Carol Misze Cox
Fort Lauderdale, FL

Redecorating

Familiarize students with a wide range of colors and color intensity. From your local paint store, obtain paint charts or color strips. Have students choose new colors for the following and write their choices:

- Redecorate your room.
- Change your eye color.
- Paint the exterior of your house.
- Dye your hair.
- Repaint your family car.
- Wallpaper the kitchen.
- Reupholster Dad's favorite chair.
- Carpet the classroom.

Make a chart to record and compare answers. Which colors are most popular? What color is a favorite with each student?

Make a list of words that have a color in them.

Color Activities

Make A Rainbow

Use any or all of these activities to create rainbows with your students.

- Place a small mirror in a glass of water, and tilt the mirror against the glass.
- Use prisms, beads, diamonds, or beveled glass to bend light rays.
- Put a drop of motor oil on a puddle of water.
- Create a sinkful of soap bubbles using dish detergent.
- Spray a fine mist of water in front of a sunny window, using a plant mister or pump hairspray bottle.

Color Days

Each day of the week, choose a color to highlight. Post a chart so children can prepare for each special day by wearing something in that color. As a group, plan ahead for a daily snack of the appropriate color.

Yellow Day	Purple Day	Red Day	Blue Day	Orange Day	Brown Day	Black-and-White Day
pineapple juice	grape juice	cranberry juice	blue popcorn balls	orange juice	chocolate pudding	milk
French vanilla	grape jelly on	apples	blueberries	carrots	peanut butter on	Oreo cookies
ice cream	crackers	strawberries		orange slices	crackers	marshmallows
lemon Jell-O	purple grapes	cherry Jell-O		orange Jell-O	hot chocolate	popcorn
					gingerbread	
					cookies	

The Artist's Corner

Cut out a large artist's palette from oaktag, and label paint spots with color activities for students to complete. Place on an easel in a corner or at an art table with materials needed. As each child completes a task, he colors the corresponding spot on his record sheet with the color code from the palette.

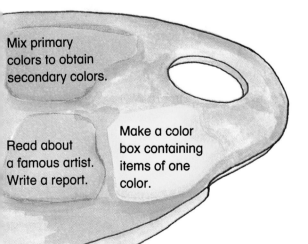

Mix primary colors to obtain secondary colors.

Read about a famous artist. Write a report.

Make a color box containing items of one color.

Color Messages

Colors can evoke feelings, symbolize ideas, and send us signals. Discuss the use of certain colors for holidays, posters, team colors, or ads. Then discuss feelings that certain colors bring out in us. Together list colors and words that we associate with them.

red
stop
danger
bloody
hot

green
fresh
lucky
go
St. Patrick's Day

yellow
warm
bright
caution
cheerful

blue
coolness
peaceful

Christmas
red and green

Halloween
orange and black

Valentine's Day
red and white

SCIENCE CORNER

OUR POLLUTED WORLD

The following are ideas for Pollution Task Cards. They may be copied or glued to 3″ × 5″ index cards.

Think about your school playground and your neighborhood. Is there noise, air, or waste pollution? Think about the type of pollution that bothers you the most. Write a slogan and design a sign to encourage people to stop polluting.

Examples:

Give a hoot. Don't pollute.

Pitch in!

Our World

If you went for a walk in the woods you might find these things on the ground. Which of these would cause pollution of the land? Why? Why don't the other things cause pollution?

branches	dead bugs	leaves
candy wrappers	acorns	tin can
foil	apple core	tire

To Do:

Bury some potato peels in your backyard.
Bury a tin can.
Mark the spot so you can check later.
What do you think will happen?
Check in a few weeks to
see if you are correct.

Sometimes we do things for a good reason, but they cause bad side effects. For example, farmers spray crops to destroy harmful insects. However, some pesticides are harmful. We need to find a better way to control pests.

To Do:

Collect newspaper and magazine articles reporting ecology and pollution problems. Write a short report explaining why we might do some things that cause pollution. Suggest a better way that would not harm our environment.

Look Up:

pesticide
insecticide

Investigate your surroundings. Select a specific location in your environment. Describe the general area and the specific site in detail. List the desirable and undesirable conditions, and propose some improvements for the area. Outline a plan of action.

Imagine being Daniel Boone living all alone in the wilderness with no neighbors nearby. Now think about a million people living in a city together. What problems are caused by so many people in a small area?

Compare your town to a pioneer settlement and write about some new problems that exist because of our modern way of living.

Explain how a visitor from another planet might describe our way of life if these were the only things he saw on a brief visit here:

1. An old junkyard
2. An empty stadium with candy wrappers, hot dog papers, and popcorn containers littered all over the empty stands
3. Overturned garbage cans in front of a brick wall, with names scrawled all over it
4. A view from the air of a very crowded housing project
5. Dead fish lying on a deserted beach

Solid Waste

How much solid waste do you throw away? You will not understand how big a problem it is to dispose of solid waste until you have some idea of how much solid waste has to be gotten rid of each day.

Make a chart on which to record what is thrown away in your home in one day. Ask each member of your family to record on the chart everything that he throws into a waste container.

Survey your friends, relatives, and neighbors to find out what they do with used bottles.

Record your results and report back to the class.

Find out the number of people living on your block. Keep a record of how many bags of garbage they put out each week for five weeks. How does the amount of garbage compare to the number of people?

Think of some constructive ways of using trash.

Noise In Your Neighborhood

On your way home from school today, try to describe ten noises you hear. Bring your list to school with you tomorrow. Now try to describe the loudness of these noises with a scale of one to ten.

Locate and record the sources of at least five of these noises. Construct a map of the area that will direct your fellow students to the approximate location of each.

Distinguish between noises which people can control and those that cannot be controlled. Design a plan for decreasing noise pollution in the area you mapped.

Going Buggy with Insects

How do you feel about creeping, crawling, hopping, flying little critters? Don't be squeamish when it comes to teaching a unit on insects! This unit is crawling with fascinating facts and exciting activities to share with your class. Don't miss the worksheet on page 138.

Diane Badden

Identifying Insects

Those pesky creatures that we lump into the category of "bugs" are really very unique. Entomologists have discovered over 800,000 kinds of insects! New varieties of insects are being discovered every day.

Have young students practice identifying insects in an animal lineup of pictures. Include pictures of insects at different stages of their development. Ask children to compare the size, habits, movement, and body parts of insects to those of other animals. After sorting out the pictures of insects, ask children to examine them closely to discover what all adult insects have in common: six legs, three main body parts, and two antennae. Then, share these interesting facts.

- The largest insect is the Goliath beetle of Africa. It grows about four inches long.
- Fossils show that insects have lived on the earth over 400 million years.
- The average number of insects in one square mile is more than all of the people on earth.
- Insects wear their skeletons on the outside of their bodies. This exoskeleton protects the insect's body like a suit of armor.
- Most insects live short lives. They become adults quickly, lay many eggs, and die.
- Insects can live almost anywhere on Earth, and they can eat almost anything.
- In South Africa, some people roast termites and eat them like popcorn!

Social Behavior

Most insects live on their own. When they are born, they are immediately responsible for their own food, shelter, and safety. Ants, termites, some bees, and some wasps, however, are social insects. They work together to care for their young, find food, and build homes. Have students observe the behavior of ants and discuss the division of labor. Ask children to name some of the benefits of living in an organized group and what humans can learn from watching insects.

Insect Territory!

Let children explore surrounding areas for insect habitats. Search the soil. Examine trees, ponds, and gardens. How about some dark corner of a cupboard, inside an old book, or on your pet? Only in the oceans are very few insects found. Have the class make a list of insect homes. Help children to conclude that insects are tough little critters that have adapted to life almost everywhere.

Turn your list of insect homes into a classroom book. Each child designs one page illustrating an insect home. Staple the pages together with a student-designed cover. Place the book where children can flip through the pages to discover unique insect homes.

Feeding Time

By looking at the mouth parts of insects, we can gather clues as to what and how they eat. Try this activity with your students to learn about the four basic types of insect mouths. Each student will need a small piece of sponge, a paper cup with juice inside, a drinking straw, and a marshmallow. You may wish to obtain a hypodermic needle and an orange for a demonstration also.

Some insects have mouths that work almost like ours. They bite and chew their food. But because insects have no teeth, they use their strong jaws and the sharp edges of their mouths to bite and chew. Have students bite and chew marshmallows like crickets, grasshoppers, roaches, mantids, dragonflies, beetles, termites, and ants.

Grasshopper

Some insects have strong mouth parts that look like a hose. They use these to suck nectar from flowers. Ask children to suck the "nectar" from their cups using the drinking straws like moths, butterflies, and bees.

Butterfly

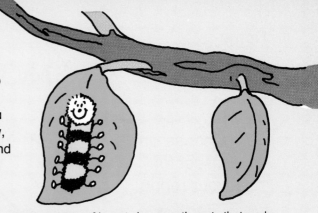

Another group of insects has mouth parts that work like a hypodermic needle. They jab their food and suck the liquid out. Demonstrate this by injecting the needle into the orange. Mosquitoes, lice, fleas, and aphids have this type of mouth.

Mosquito

A few insects have mouth parts that they use to soak up liquids like a sponge. Have students use pieces of sponge to soak up any juice left in their cups. The common housefly has a mouth like this.

Housefly

Helpful or Harmful?

Prepare for a vote on the "Insect Issue." Discuss and list the advantages and disadvantages of insects. Organize a Bug Rally in your classroom. Divide the class into pro- and anti-bug teams. Students make posters and give speeches to share their ideas. Invite knowledgeable community members to discuss insects with the class: farmer, pest-control worker, entomologist, insect collector.

Practice categorizing helpful and harmful insects. Remember that some insects could be in both groups. Termites, for example, destroy wooden structures, but they also clean up decayed wood on the forest floor. Finally, take a vote.

Advantages: eat other harmful insects; pollinate plants; eat dead organisms; cultivate the soil; produce honey, beeswax, and silk; provide food for birds, reptiles, amphibians, fish and other animals

Disadvantages: spread disease; destroy crops, trees, and plantlife; make life difficult for humans and animals; scare us

Eviction Notices For Insect Pests

Why are insect infestations so difficult to control? Insects have survived many years on our changing Earth because of their small size, their body structure, and their ability to reproduce in great numbers. In addition, they have techniques of escaping from enemies, communicating with their own species, and adapting to hostile environments.

Have students write paragraphs from the point of view of insect tenants who have just been evicted and are looking for a new home. What kind of environments would they prefer as insects? Have students role-play the stories of a grasshopper, mosquito, housefly, roach, and moth who are under attack by humans. What are their reactions to insecticides, flyswatters, mothballs, mosquito spray, and "roach motels"?

My Insect Report

Choose an insect for your report.

Then complete these sentences.

My Insect Report

My report is about the _____.

This insect has _____ legs, _____ wings, and

_____ antennae. It lives _____

_____. This insect likes to eat _____

_____.

Something interesting about this insect is _____

_____.

It can also _____

_____. It is _____
helpful or harmful

to man because it _____.

This insect is about the same size as a _____

_____.

Bonus Box: Draw a picture of this insect on the back of this paper. Show where it lives.

Piggy Bank Power

Introduce primary students to beginning money skills with these activities.

The Coin Thief

To practice coin recognition and money words, make large flash cards or overhead transparencies of the front and back of each of the following: penny, nickel, dime, and quarter. Write the words quarter, dime, nickel, and penny on the board. Have each child make his own set of word cards labeled with these words. The teacher says, "This is a holdup. Stick 'em up!" The children hold up word cards to match the coin she is holding. To vary, hold up value cards which say 25¢, 10¢, 5¢, or 1¢.

Mary Dinneen
Bristol, CT

Money Counts!

Lead into counting nickels and dimes with this bounce-ball game. Have students stand in a circle. One player starts counting to five. As he says, "Five," he bounces the ball and passes it to the next person who says, "Ten." Players continue bouncing the ball and counting by fives around the circle. If a player counts incorrectly or drops the ball, he steps into the center of the circle until another person takes his place. (Vary the game by counting by tens. Or count by ones and tell children not to bounce the ball on multiples of five.)

Mary Dinneen

Bank Clerks

As classroom bank clerks, children will learn to organize coins from highest to lowest values. Each child makes a cash drawer from an empty egg carton by labeling the inside with coin names. Provide paper coins or play money. The child separates his coins into the proper egg cups. Student partners take turns being bank customer and clerk. The customer asks the clerk for various coins (i.e., two dimes, one nickel, three pennies). The clerk arranges the coins from highest to lowest value on his desk and then counts the money.

Mary Dinneen

Money Kits

Use a small box and money cards to provide individual practice in counting money. Cover the box with Con-Tact paper and label it "Money Kit." Make money cards by stamping various coin amounts on tagboard cards. If you do not have coin stamps, cut and paste coins from old math workbooks. Limit each kit to ten different amounts. Number the cards on the back, and provide a numbered worksheet and answer key. The student counts the amount of money shown on each card and writes the total on the worksheet.

Dartha Williamson
Athens, GA

It's Money In The Bank!

Put money in the bank with coin stamps to practice making given amounts. Cut out several tagboard piggy banks. Laminate and use a wipe-off marker to program each pig with a money amount. Provide rubber money stamps and a stamp pad. Children stamp the correct coins to make the amounts shown. Assign a student banker to see that each child's savings equal the amount on his bank. If correct, children wipe off answers and trade piggy banks. Change the amounts on the piggy banks as your students' skills improve.

Mary Anne T. Haffner
Waynesboro, PA

Planning For Successful Parent Conferences

Planning ahead for parent conferences can help you avoid tense moments and preconference jitters. Try these teacher-tested tips to establish a friendly atmosphere and positive attitudes.

● During parent-teacher conference week, I purchase a bouquet of flowers and place them on the table where I hold my conferences. It adds a colorful touch and a delightful scent while setting a pleasant tone for both parents and myself.

Pamela Myhowich
Auburn, WA

● I have parents sit at a reading table with me during the conference. Before conferences, I cover the table with yellow butcher paper and let two children at a time come to the table to write and decorate a message for their parents. This table covering has started many conferences on a pleasant note. Parents enjoy searching for their child's message.

Pamela Myhowich

● When preparing for conferences, place paper and pens at the table. This allows the teacher to jot down parents' questions, as well as enabling parents to take notes freely.

Joyce Hodge
Orange Park, FL

● Make sure your seat and the parents' seats are equal height and not on opposite sides of a desk. This reduces intimidating feelings.

Antoinette Murphy
Sidman, PA

● Create a warm, inviting environment to reduce nervousness:
Play soothing classical music in the background.
Put fresh flowers or a silk flower arrangement at the table.
Light a scented candle and keep it burning during the conference.
Position a lamp and comfortable chairs.
Have the child's best art project or a special paper ready in a folder.

Sr. Ann Claire Rhoads

● At your school's Open House, hang a sign-up sheet for conferences. Pencil in dates and times. Parents get to indicate the times which would be most convenient for them. This is a tremendous help with scheduling parent conferences.

Joyce Hodge

● When parents enter my classroom, I give them a tour of the room. I focus on the work that their child has done individually as well as in cooperation with his or her classmates. This brief tour gives parents a chance to warm up to the school environment and the teacher.

Antoinette Murphy

● If you have a set conference schedule, you can provide this special introduction to each conference. Tape-record student responses to one or more questions: How is school going so far? How do you think you are doing? Tell something good that you do to help the class. Videotape students if possible. Each parent hears only his or her child.

Sr. Ann Claire Rhoads, Emmitsburg, MD

- The day before conferences, my students make cookies. I put these out with a fresh pot of coffee, tea, or hot cocoa to welcome parents.

  Linda Crissman, Gratis, OH

- I display photographs of my students taken during a Halloween party or other event to provide enjoyment for parents who are waiting to meet the teacher. I move my class easel into the hall, mount the photos, and add a title.

  Coreen Stamper, Cleveland, OH

- I use a post-conference form in my files. This tells me who attended the conference, what topics were discussed, what the parents' comments or concerns were, and the actions which were agreed upon.

  Cindy Edwards, Vernon Hills, IL

- Try to end each conference on an optimistic note. Parents should leave with a hopeful feeling. Positive attitudes and your suggestions can help parents help their children.

  Deborah Gardner, Trenton, NJ

- I make a take-home library. I list the materials that parents and children can borrow on a one-week basis. Each game or activity is numbered and coordinates with a take-home library card. At conference time, I check off a list of materials that would help each parent help his or her child.

  Helen Salamone, Delmar, NY

- Provide old worksheets and workbooks in boxes labeled according to subjects. Let parents choose from these for their children to use as reinforcement at home. While the parents are waiting to talk with you, they can pick up worksheets on the subjects indicated on their students' work folders.

  Mary F. Williams, Miamisburg, OH

- Prior to conference time, send home a survey for each parent to complete and return at the conference. This helps parents examine their child's education and prepare for the conference. (Some sample questions are: What do you feel is your child's best subject? What do you think is your child's weakest subject? How does your child feel about school?) Add questions to the survey that pertain to your class.

  Sharleen Berg, Red Wing, MN

- I often come across articles in magazines or newspapers which deal with current issues in education: homework, retention, school difficulties. I cut these out and keep them in a folder. If a parent has questions about one of these subjects at a conference, I give the article to the parent as he leaves. He can stop by the office to make a copy and put the original in my mailbox.

  Carole Pippert, Bowie, MD

Freddy's Guide to
Good Nutrition

Kids can really sink their teeth into this nutrition unit! See the worksheets on pages 143 and 144.

Ideas by Sharon Haley

Hors D'Oeuvres

Make nutrition an ongoing study in your room. Select a volunteer to be the "chef of the week." Provide the ingredients and supplies, and have the chef demonstrate preparation of a nutritious snack for the class. Then have students prepare their own snacks. Before eating, discuss the ingredients and nutritional value. Extend the activity by having students copy the recipes in their best handwriting. Collect the recipes each week, and have students make them into a cookbook to be given to their mothers for Mother's Day.

Johnny Appleseed Sandwiches
apples (sliced)
crunchy peanut butter
Spread peanut butter on an apple slice. Top with another slice of apple.
Enjoy!

Wormy, Squirmy Snacks
toothpicks
cherry tomatoes
raisins
celery leaves
Attach three cherry tomatoes together using toothpicks. Break a toothpick in half. With each half, attach a raisin eye. Add celery leaf antennae. Dig in!

Fruit Delight
canned pear halves
prunes
mandarin orange segments
maraschino cherries
raisins
Arrange as shown.

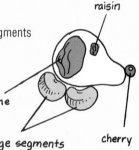

raisin

prune

orange segments

cherry

Ingredients Á La Carte

Amaze your students by introducing them to the ingredients in the foods they eat. Encourage them to bring labels and containers that would otherwise be discarded. Examine the ingredient lists together to determine the nutritional value of foods. Remind students that ingredients are listed in order according to quantity. What is the main ingredient? Is it sugar? How does the ingredient list of one brand compare to another? Creating a new awareness about ingredients could promote better nutritional habits among your students.

An Apple A Day

Colorful, apple-shaped diaries are an excellent starting point for examining students' eating habits. Trace an apple outline and duplicate on red and white construction paper. Have students cut out two red and five white apples. Using the red apples as covers, staple all seven apples together to make a booklet. Ask students to write "My Diet" and their name on the front of the booklet. Then have them label the pages "Monday" through "Friday." As they note their diets for the week, ask them to categorize the foods according to the four food groups. Also, have them list low-nutritional-value foods that they eat, such as carbonated drinks and chips.

Make a bulletin board showing four grocery bags and a trash can. Label bags milk, meat, fruit–vegetable, and grain. From students' booklets, list the foods your class consumed during the week. List the low-nutritional-value foods on the trash can. Discuss the results.

Freddy's Guide To Fine Dining

Freddy was in a hurry to finish his book.
He forgot capital letters and punctuation marks.
Capitalize and punctuate the sentences.

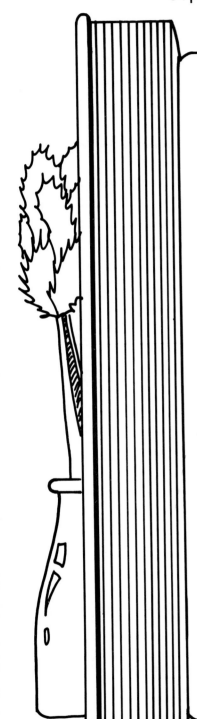

1. never eat anything that s on fire

2. only snack between meals

3. always check your walnuts for squirrels

4. don t save your dessert for last eat it first

5. never leave your food dish under a bird cage

6. chew food at least once

7. only play in your food if you ve already eaten your toys

8. don t eat nuts you are what you eat

9. eat every meal as though it were your last

10. all this eating and sleeping can wear a guy down

Bonus Box: Write five more silly dining rules on the back of this page. Draw a picture for each one.

Name _____

On The Road To Good Nutrition

Read and complete each box on your Road to Good Nutrition.

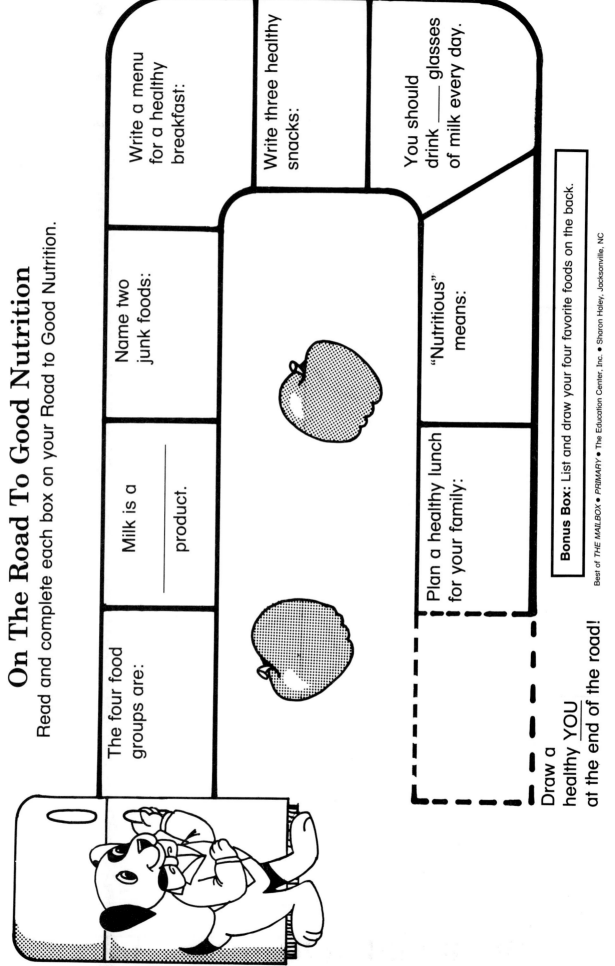

The four food groups are:

Milk is a _____ product.

Name two junk foods:

Write a menu for a healthy breakfast:

Write three healthy snacks:

You should drink ___ glasses of milk every day.

"Nutritious" means:

Plan a healthy lunch for your family:

Draw a healthy YOU at the end of the road!

Bonus Box: List and draw your four favorite foods on the back.

Best of *THE MAILBOX* • *PRIMARY* • The Education Center, Inc. • Sharon Haley, Jacksonville, NC

A CARNIVAL TO REMEMBER

When we issued an S.O.S. for suggestions for putting on an exciting school carnival, our readers responded by sending us loads of terrific ideas! Share these planning tips and fun activities with your parent-teacher organization. Everyone will agree that "this year's carnival was the best ever!"

- Good planning is crucial to holding a successful carnival. Choose the carnival date as quickly as possible to avoid scheduling conflicts. Set goals and target dates. Form committees to plan each aspect: advertising and publicity; food and refreshments; decorating; games and booths; prizes; cleanup; ticket sales; demonstrations and displays. Start early and start smart!

- Involve students by scheduling each classroom to "man" a booth or game. Even young children can help award prizes or hand out refreshments. Enlist the aid of local scout troops to help sell programs, direct parking, clean up, or serve as "runners" on carnival day.

- Baby-sitting services at your carnival will encourage entire families to attend. Set up a baby-sitting room in your school. Ask parents or local 4-H Club members to volunteer as sitters.

- Carnival programs will bring in a big profit and help your guests make the most of their time. Include a schedule of events, a map of the carnival grounds, and a list of merchants who donated prizes or supplies. Canvass your community and PTA for businesses that might advertise in the program. Save printing costs by using your school's copier.

- Ask area businesses to sponsor a classroom! Sponsorship could include use of office duplicating machines or donations of money, equipment, or prizes for the carnival. Give sponsors free advertising space in the carnival program. Students could tour the sponsor's business and learn about its operation. Employees might volunteer time at the carnival or in the classroom, or donate items for an auction. Everyone will benefit from these perfect partnerships!

- Using tickets instead of money at the carnival eliminates the hassle of making change. Sell tickets in advance and at the carnival. Encourage early sales by selling advance tickets at a lower price. Ask a local bank to supply envelopes for each classroom. Teachers can seal tickets for each student to sell in an envelope for a safe journey home.

- Advertising your carnival will create interest and ensure large, enthusiastic crowds. Submit written releases to your school, community, and city newspapers. Be sure to include important information about the event (who, what, where, why, when, and how much) and a phone number to call for more details. Write short announcements to broadcast on radio and television at least three weeks prior to the carnival. Make posters, signs, handbills, and flyers. Ask local businesses to display your announcements. Post banners at school events, or drape one across your school building. And don't forget to talk it up! Word of mouth is still one of the best means of advertising. Get the word out!

- Prizes for each game should be gathered well in advance. Ask local businesses for donations. Volunteers can make inexpensive prizes over the summer. Sock and stick puppets are popular with kids and adults. Purchase inexpensive tube socks in both your school colors and remate them. Use the "school spirit socks" as prizes, or sell them at a booth. Try awarding combs, stickers, sugarless candy, balloons, pencils, bookmarks, fast-food coupons, or discount movie tickets. For easy display, use curtain hooks and chicken wire to hang stuffed animal prizes.

If your carnival activities generate more yawns than yippees, read on!

Shirt Stand

Sell T-shirts printed with your school's logo or mascot. Let children add personal designs with fabric crayons, glitter, and sequins.

Chalk Walk

Sell tickets for a chance to turn the school sidewalk into a work of art! Have children and adults work together with chalk to decorate sidewalk squares. Award prizes before the close of the carnival.

Bicycle Parade

Ask a local police officer to give a short talk on bike safety. Then let children decorate their bikes with crepe paper. Make an announcement during the carnival, and hold a parade around the school grounds.

Petting Farm

Ask your local 4-H Club to bring small farm animals to your carnival. Provide straw and set up your petting farm on the playground or parking lot. Be sure to limit the number of children with the animals at one time.

Beautiful Balloons

Set up a "design-a-balloon" stand. Provide a large supply of helium-filled balloons, sequins, glitter, permanent magic markers, stickers, and glue. Children pay to decorate a balloon—an inexpensive souvenir of a fun day!

Face And Body Painting

Even adults will enjoy the fun of a face-painting booth. To prepare the paint, mix 1 teaspoon of hand lotion into each pint bottle of tempera paint (regular and fluorescent). Multiply the fun by adding glitter, sequins, small beads, or salt colored with food coloring to painted faces. Older children will enjoy being painted like their favorite rock star or having messages "tattooed" on their arms and legs.

Cupcake Creations

Kids will line up for the chance to decorate (and eat!) their own cupcake creations. Place cupcakes and tubes for cake icing on a table. Participants decorate their cupcakes using gumdrops, licorice, pretzels, colored sugar, and other small candies. For easy eating, place finished cupcakes in ice cream cones!

Popcorn Plus

Don't hesitate to be creative with everyone's favorite snack! Pack a popcorn stand with various flavored popcorns. Sprinkle popped corn with Parmesan cheese, chili powder, bacon-flavored bits, grated American cheese, or garlic salt.

Goldfish Pond

For a prize that's a winner every time, try a goldfish "pond." Contact a local pet store about purchasing approximately 300 goldfish. (Most stores are eager to sell the fish at cost in exchange for free advertising at the carnival.) Place the fish in a small wading pool. Provide several small fishing nets and quart-size freezer bags. Allow children to catch their own prize. (Be sure to give reluctant parents the option of choosing another prize for their child.) Help new pet owners by posting a sign telling where to purchase fish supplies.

Displays And Demonstrations

Ask community resource people to set up displays or hold demonstrations for carnival-goers. Some demonstrations to try this year: karate, gymnastics, juggling, magic, first aid, pet care, weaving, pottery, dance, mime. Invite local police, fire, and ambulance personnel to answer questions. Children and adults will enjoy examining the various emergency vehicles on display.

Funny Photo Booth

What child doesn't love having his picture taken? To prepare this booth, paint different figures on large pieces of cardboard: a sports figure, cheerleader, animal, clown, rock star. Cut out the face of each figure. Each child stands behind one of the figures, places his head through the cut-out oval, and has his photo taken. Be sure to use an instant camera so kids can take their pictures home with them.

Pick-a-Pocket Clown

Here's a money-maker that's perfect for younger children. Have a volunteer dress in a clown costume with several numbered pockets. Children redeem a ticket for the chance to pick a prize from one of the clown's pockets.

The Master Of The Locks

Hang several locks from a board. Place the keys to the locks on a key ring. Challenge players to open all the locks within a certain time limit. Be sure to award a small prize to all players, whether they "beat the clock" or not.

Good Luck Ducks

Fill a small wading pool with water. Paint a number on the bottom of each of several plastic ducks. Place the ducks in the pool. Each child picks a duck from the pool and wins a prize labeled with the corresponding number.

Sponge Toss

What a joy to toss a wet sponge at a favorite teacher! Have each volunteer teacher place her head in an inner tube. Let children toss soft, wet sponges at the good-natured target.

Coin Toss

For a challenging game, place 20–25 six-packs of soda pop (bottom side up) in a small, plastic wading pool. Children toss dimes in the pool from behind a barrier. (A table turned over on its side works great.) Players earn a prize for each dime that lands on top of a can. Add extra excitement by taping dollar bills to a few of the cans. If your carnival is indoors, place the pool on plastic sheeting so the dimes won't roll all over the floor.

Treasure Hunt

Fill a large box with Styrofoam packing chips. Hide small prizes and candy in the chips. Children place one hand in the box and pull out a surprise!

Sock It To A Teacher!

This booth will be quite a hit with the students! Have each teacher draw or paint her face on a sock. Place each sock on a bottle (labeled with the teacher's name). The player redeems a ticket for the chance to throw a ball at his favorite teacher.

Kathy Beard Melrose, FL	Martha Herin Madison, IN	Jane Scott Mebane, NC
Sandra Docca Silver Spring, MD	Dormalee H. Lindberg Carbondale, IL	Mary Wisser Anaheim, CA
Rebecca L. Gibson Auburn, AL	Mrs. Jeff Marcuson Elwood, IN	Sr. Margaret Ann Wooden Martinsburg, WV
Sr. Ann Claire Rhoads Emmitsburg, MD	Our thanks to these contributors to this article.	

Opening Night!

It's that time of the year again—Open House Night at your school! New students, new teachers, new parents!

Invitations have been sent out. A new cast is assembled. The scene is set. Classrooms are decorated with students' work, and desks are clean and tidy. The staff waits anxiously in the wings.

What's in store when school doors open to the inquisitive crowds? Be prepared for rave reviews when you use these Open House ideas!

Me Mobiles

Decorate the room with "Me Mobiles" hanging from the ceiling. Each student writes his name on a piece of colored construction paper. Children slip the colored papers over their hangers and attach items that describe themselves or things that they enjoy.

Paula K. Holdren
Prospect, KY

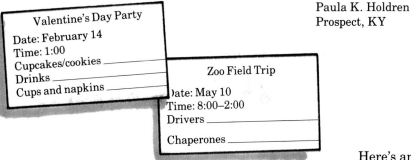

Sign Up, Please!

Looking for parent volunteers for field trips, class parties, and clerical tasks? Design a display that they can't miss at Open House! Place an attractive booklet and several pens in an area of the classroom. Invite parents to sign up for the jobs they would like. It will save you countless hours on the telephone searching for last-minute help.

Who Am I?

Here's an intriguing way to get parents involved at Open House. It also helps students to get acquainted. Put student names in a hat, and have classmates draw names. Each child then sketches his classmate and writes five clues to his or her identity. Post the drawings with clues on the bulletin board, and hide the name of each student subject under a flap. Parents will have fun guessing which child is theirs!

Paula K. Holdren

Class Video Stars

Videotape a class play or lesson to play back on Open House Night. The kids will love the experience of being on TV and will beg their parents to come see the video show. Each child is involved, and parents will leave smiling after seeing their "little ones" on TV!

Francine Reinel
Sarasota, FL

Open House Invitation

Write an invitation to Open House on the board. Use it as a handwriting assignment. Children will do their best when they know it's going home to Mom and Dad!

Kathy Beard
Keystone Heights, FL

Welcome Parents and Friends

Hang a large sign outside your door to welcome visitors. Each child signs his name to welcome family members and friends to their special night at school.

Joan Holesko
North Tonawanda, NY

Student Dummies?

Welcome parents with a classroom full of student dummies! Have each child lie down on a piece of butcher paper. Trace around him, and let him color and cut out his outline. Put each outlined form in the child's desk. Will parents be able to find their child's place?

Kathy Beard

A Welcoming Committee of One

If your Open House comes in the fall, a scarecrow may be just the thing to welcome family and friends to your classroom. Students will have fun building a scarecrow from an old lamp stand and adding clothes stuffed with straw or newspaper. Let classmates name their class mascot. Give him a sign, place him by the door to welcome guests, and add a few pumpkins at his feet. Visitors can't miss your classroom with this charming fellow to meet and greet them!

Lynda Holding
Blanchard, OK

All About Me

As they present these books to parents at Open House, children can proudly say, "Here's a book all about me!" Watch as children and parents sit down to turn the pages together. Have students begin work on their books on the first day of school. Each day, hand out pages for children to fill in with information about themselves. Topics may include: Interests, Favorites, Special Feelings, Dreams, Things That Bug Me, My Autobiography, Family Tree, Places I Have Lived, Places I Have Visited, Family, School, and Weekends. Bind each student's pages together to make a unique book and a special gift that is sure to impress parents.

Julia K. Mozingo
Altus, OK

Silhouette Riddles

A display of classroom silhouettes will attract parents' attention. Use an overhead projector to create each child's silhouette on black paper. Cut out and mount these on white paper. Have each child write a riddle about himself. Mount riddles beside cutouts. Parents will have fun finding their child's likeness by shape and riddle.

Clara Presutti
Wheeling, WV

OUR READERS WRITE

Shhhhh...

Ask your favorite carpeting store to save samples from discontinued styles and colors. These fit nicely on children's desks. They are very handy (and quiet) when children are using puzzles or other noisy items. They also keep things from rolling off flat desktops.

Fran Petersen
North Tonawanda, NY

Be A Good Egg

Decorate your room and instruct your students at the same time with large eggs cut from colored paper. Provide an assortment of lace, ribbon, sequins, flowers, etc. Let your students decorate the eggs and think up appropriate messages to promote good behavior or other desirable character traits.

Fran Petersen

Change-O

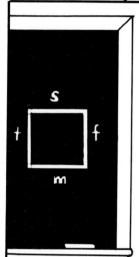

Draw a square on your chalkboard. Print a letter or word on each side as illustrated. Have the children look carefully at the board and then close their eyes. Erase one letter or word and change it. Call on a student to tell what has been changed. Example: You changed the letter *f* to a capital *M*, or you changed the word "them" to "there." This is also a good review with numbers.

Clean-up Fun

After an art project, when the floor is littered with scraps of paper, we play "Scrap Race." I'll say a color, and all the children must pick up only scraps of that color and put them on their table. Then I'll call another color and only those colored scraps may be picked up and placed on the table. This goes on until all scraps are gone, and the table with the largest pile of scraps wins. The winners are allowed to go to lunch first or get an extra five minutes of play. This really helps to get all the mess cleaned up quickly while reinforcing color recognition.

Lynn Klomfar
Gulfport, FL

Candy Game Markers

Make games even more enticing by using colorful, wrapped candy pieces as game markers. Players will be delighted that they may eat their markers at the conclusion of the game.

Elizabeth Cole
Annapolis, MD

Cinder-Block Wall Display

A few brads and a roll of tape work like magic for displaying children's work on cinder-block walls. Bend one prong of each brad upward to form a hook. Tape the "hooks" on the wall, punch holes in the children's work, and hang!

Peggy C. Vice
New Iberia, LA

Lollipop Plant

Use a spare plant as a gift for a sick child. Insert ten to 15 straws around the plant; then put lollipops in them. Wrap with aluminum foil and add a bow.

Connie Connely
Catoosa, OK

Yazoo The Yardstick

Children can make their own colorful yardsticks by pasting 36 one-inch circles on a tagboard strip. To show the divisions by foot, make the 12th, 24th, and 36th circles of a contrasting color. When completed, children can use their yardsticks to measure objects around the room. Younger children might enjoy a story about Yazoo meeting his friends (circles) and special friends (contrasting colors).

Joan Blanco
Pompano Beach, FL

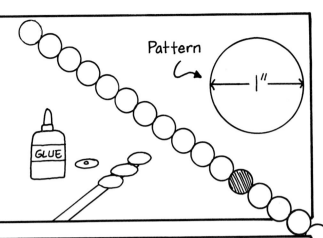
Pattern
1"
GLUE

First-Day Friends

For a welcome warm-up on the first day of school, cut squares from colored paper and slash each square into two irregular shapes. As you greet each child, ask him to choose a shape. After everyone has arrived, have each child find the person with the shape that completes his square. Then let the "new friends" get acquainted for a few minutes. Try this for a few days until everyone has met.

Annette Mathias
Partridge, KS

All Kinds Of Things

Spark creative thinking, and provide extra credit with "quick lists." Write a topic or category on a 3″×5″ card. Each student selects a card and lists at least five items for that category. Give an award to the child who lists the most items for a specific category. Sample lists may include things found in the sky, kinds of tools, things with wheels, things you can do in winter, and types of buildings.

Lori Schmidt
Lima, OH

Reusable Birthday Cake

Mix ½-box (13-ounce size) Ivory Snow flakes with water and food coloring. When mixture begins to stiffen, add 2–3 tablespoons alum to cause hardening later. Cover the outside of an inverted plastic bowl with the mixture, as if icing a cake; then add decorations and candles. The "cake" will harden in two to three hours and can be used over and over again.

Sister M. Henrietta
Bayonne, NJ

Daily Bow Ties

To teach days of the week, label and display a teddy bear cutout for each day. Punch holes and string yarn as shown. Each morning a student will dress the teddy of the day by tying his bow tie.

Margaret Paris
Leesville, LA

Monday

Subscription Cards

Stop throwing away those annoying magazine subscription cards and start collecting them. Give to children for a fun lesson in writing their names and addresses. Be sure to cross out the backs of the cards so they can't be mailed!

Becky Cebula
Elkton, MD

Name:_____
Address:_____
City:___ State:___
Home phone:_____

Question Jar

My class "question jar" is a great way to fill odd minutes at the end of class or review basic facts before a test. I write increasingly difficult questions to put in the jar as the year progresses. Humorous questions are a nice break from academic ones, on occasion. A student draws a question and answers it. If he is correct, I reward him with a sticker or applause from the rest of the class.

Linda Brewer
Ivanhoe, TX

Gifts For Parents

Have students frame their most prized artwork to give to their parents at Christmas. You'll need a greeting card box, an artwork sample, craft glue, and rickrack or ribbon for each student. Have each student cut his artwork to fit in the bottom of the box and glue in place. Use an X-acto knife to cut an opening in the cover of each box. Have students paint the box covers if necessary for an attractive frame and glue on rickrack or ribbon. These frames also make a great display for students' school pictures with a few lines of poetry.

Sr. Ann Claire Rhoads
Emmitsburg, MD

Puppet Show Table

Turn an ordinary worktable into an instant puppet stage. Lay a square or rectangular table on its side and place student puppeteers behind it. Great for all of your class puppet shows.

Barbara Sellberg
Bristol, CT

Mobile Centers

I've found a new use for two old wagons I bought at a garage sale—mobile learning centers! I've turned mine into math and reading centers, and used them to hold a Halloween poetry display. They're also perfect for carrying encyclopedias during report writing.

Eleanor Messner
Dalton, PA

Christmas Hints

Shortly after Thanksgiving, I make up a list of educational materials and games that can be purchased in the local department stores. I list the materials according to skills and send it home to parents. The list gives ideas about materials that can help their children and is very helpful before the holiday season.

Sandra McGahey
Belleville, MI

Ideal File

Over the summer I organize all the ideas I have gathered from magazines during the school year. Using a three-ring notebook, dividers labeled with subject headings, scissors, and glue, I reread my magazines, clipping articles and placing them in the correct sections. Then, during the school year when I need an idea, I remove the appropriate page from my notebook, clip it in my plan book, and go. When I try an idea, I often jot down my results or variations for the next time around.

Lois Cooper
Beckley, WV

Valentine List

Children can make a valentine list to take home by alphabetizing their classmates' names. About two weeks before Valentine's Day, have students write their names with dark crayons on 4" × 18" strips of paper. As a class, arrange these strips in columns, one for boys and one for girls, and alphabetize by last name. Children then copy the names on a valentine worksheet complete with the teacher's name and a special note to parents.

Mary Dinneen
Bristol, CT

Noodle Coloring

Whenever we do a project with macaroni noodles, I color the noodles first, using Easter egg–coloring packages. The noodles come out with bright coloring—ready to string, sort, count, etc.

Eleanor Messner
Dalton, PA

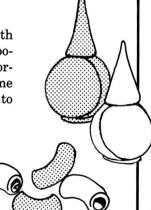

Flying Witches

For a cute Halloween party decoration, draw a simple outline of a witch and cut it out of black construction paper. With a hole punch, make two holes at the bottom edge of the witch and slide in a lollipop with the candy part at the back. With the sucker in place, the witch looks like she is riding her broomstick across the sky! See the pattern.

Joan Holesko
North Tonawanda, NY

Pattern

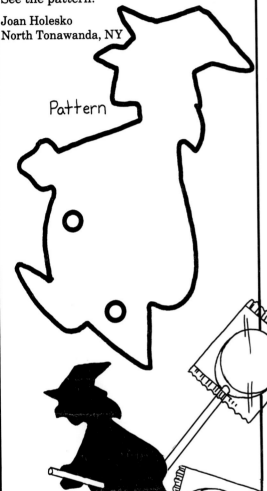

State Study Latchhook

Students get hooked on this class project. Use an overhead projector to copy the outline, rivers, and major highways of your state on latchhook canvas. My class hooked the state green, rivers blue, and highways red to fill the design. We presented it to our state senator in the capitol, and it hangs in his office.

Beverly Strayer
Red Lion, PA

Lima Beans

Write numbers or letters on large, dried lima beans with a fine-line marker and coat with clear acrylic spray. Use these beans for practice in learning alphabetical order, numerical order, or word blends, or for practicing spelling words. Uses are endless and kids will love the "bean box."

Sharon Gullett
Tyler, TX

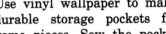

Wallpaper Pockets

Use vinyl wallpaper to make durable storage pockets for game pieces. Sew the pocket on a sewing machine and add a strap to keep flap tucked in. Easy to make, easy to write on, easy to clean!

Donna Bjorklund
Shakopee, MN

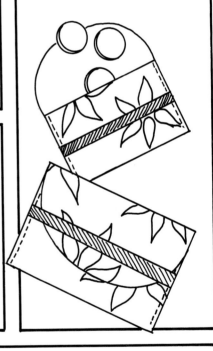

Workbook Corners

My first and second graders have difficulty finding pages quickly. When they complete a workbook page and I finish checking it, I trim the corner. The children can then turn right to the next assignment.

Margaret Leyen
Iowa Falls, IA

Cat Tales and Scary Stories

Have children write Halloween tales and decorate them with imaginative art. Mount stories on light-colored construction paper. Add tails, ears, hats, or anything to give away the topic.

Sr. Ann Claire Rhoads
Emmitsburg, MD

Class Crosswords

Make up a name crossword puzzle about your class using your students' first names. Have each student supply a clue about himself. For example, "I was born in Detroit and have two older sisters."

Melissa Noonkester Matusevich
Christiansburg, VA

Name Tag Puzzle

To break the ice on the first day of school, make a name tag puzzle for each child. On a piece of poster board 3″ × 6″ or larger, write a child's name with a broad-tip marker. You may also add other decorations to the card—flowers, kites, balloons, etc. Laminate the card. With scissors cut the card into several pieces, depending on the level of your students. Keep the puzzle in an envelope with the child's name on it. On the first day of school put each envelope on the desk where you want the child to sit. As the children come in, they can amuse themselves by working their own puzzles. Later you may let them trade and work each other's. Ultimately, they can be taken home.

Barbara Dixon
Loveland, OH

Laminating Cutouts

Having problems with cut-out pictures not holding up? Laminate them, but leave a wide edge of laminating film around each one when trimming. This makes the edges strong and keeps small pieces from getting torn off or lost.

Rebecca L. Gibson
Auburn, AL

Rubber Cement Trick

Instead of using Velcro or magnetic tape on matching activities, put a drop of rubber cement on the back of each piece and let dry. You can press the piece to the activity and it will stick, but it will also be easy to remove. Rub the rubber cement off, and replace after a month's use.

Nancy Farlow
St. Joseph, MO

Flash Cards

I like to use flash cards in different shapes, such as this dinosaur card. Laminate shapes to use again throughout the year or to accompany a special unit.

Margaret Leyen
Iowa Falls, IA

Sponge Dice

Instead of using regular dice in your learning games, cut cubes out of sponges and label the sides with numbers or dots. Not only are sponge dice cheaper—they're quieter too!

Diana McGuckin
Kankakee, IL

Quiet Clean-up Time

To shorten and quiet down desk clean-out time, set a timer for about three to five minutes. Challenge the children to see if they can all finish before the timer rings, working so quietly they can hear it ticking as they work.

Fran Petersen
North Tonawanda, NY

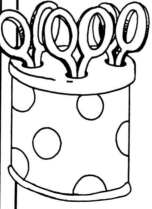

Scissor Keeper

Here's a way to keep the children's scissors neat and untangled on the shelf. Take a clean, wide, flat can, like a peanut can, and cover it around the outside with colorful Con-Tact paper. Place the can bottom-side up, so that the open end is down. Take a bottle opener and punch out holes around the entire closed end. Scissors can now be placed in these holes in a neat and orderly fashion.

D'Leigh Harvell
Atlanta, GA

All Mixed-up

Students of any age will enjoy this alphabetical order game. On one side of the chalkboard, list all your students' first names. On the other side, list all the last names. The students take a piece of paper and first list all the first names in ABC order. Then they start at the top and beside the first names, they list all the last names in ABC order. Boys and girls are really tickled in finding their new mixed-up names.

Lynne Willis
Augusta, GA

Water Spelling

I have found a way to reinforce spelling skills and clean the chalkboard at the same time. I select three children who have worked the hardest at their seats. Each student is given a small tub of water and an oval sponge. After dipping the sponge in water and squeezing, the children practice spelling and writing their words with water. Soon our chalkboard is clean!

Connie Connely
Tulsa, OK

Color Clocks

To help my students to learn to tell time, I draw a large clock with the numbers in red. Around the outside of the clock, I write the minutes in blue. Then I attach a short red hand for the hours and a long blue one for the minutes. As I show the children how to write down the time, I use the same color-coding, writing the hour in red and the minutes in blue. As the children master telling time, go to a traditional one-color clock. It works!

Geraldine Fossett
Canton, GA

Dots Made Easy

To make dots for matching number games cheaply and easily, use a new pencil eraser and a stamp pad.

Joyce Timm
Bangor, WI

Metal Washers

Small metal washers can give a game a new dimension. Glue them on your gameboard and laminate right over the top. Attach a piece of magnetic tape to each playing piece. Hang your game on a wall or bulletin board, and your game pieces will stick to the game.

Diana Leibrandt, Imperial, NE,

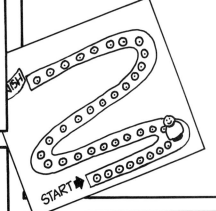

Mastering Map Skills

One of the best interest centers I ever had was the simplest! For a unit in map skills, I had the students trace the map shape on large paper using the overhead projector. After all lines and marks are traced, the student finishes the map by adding details and coloring it in. This is good for hand-eye coordination, and it helps students remember the parts of their maps.

Pat Packard
Berea, OH

Prescription Bottles

Collect prescription bottles and refill with medicine to improve spelling. Have students write spelling rules on small sheets of paper, fold the papers, and place them inside the bottles. Label each bottle with a sticker that says, "Take as needed for good spelling."

Connie Connely
Catoosa, OK

Baseball Bear
Pattern

Here's a center that acts as its own reward. Run off copies of the bear's body programmed with directions and skill information, such as the plurals used here. When the students correctly complete the work, they receive the bear head to cut out and paste on his body. The completed bears make a nice bulletin board display, and the idea can easily be adapted to other animals and skills.

Claudia Wilcox
Vernon, CT

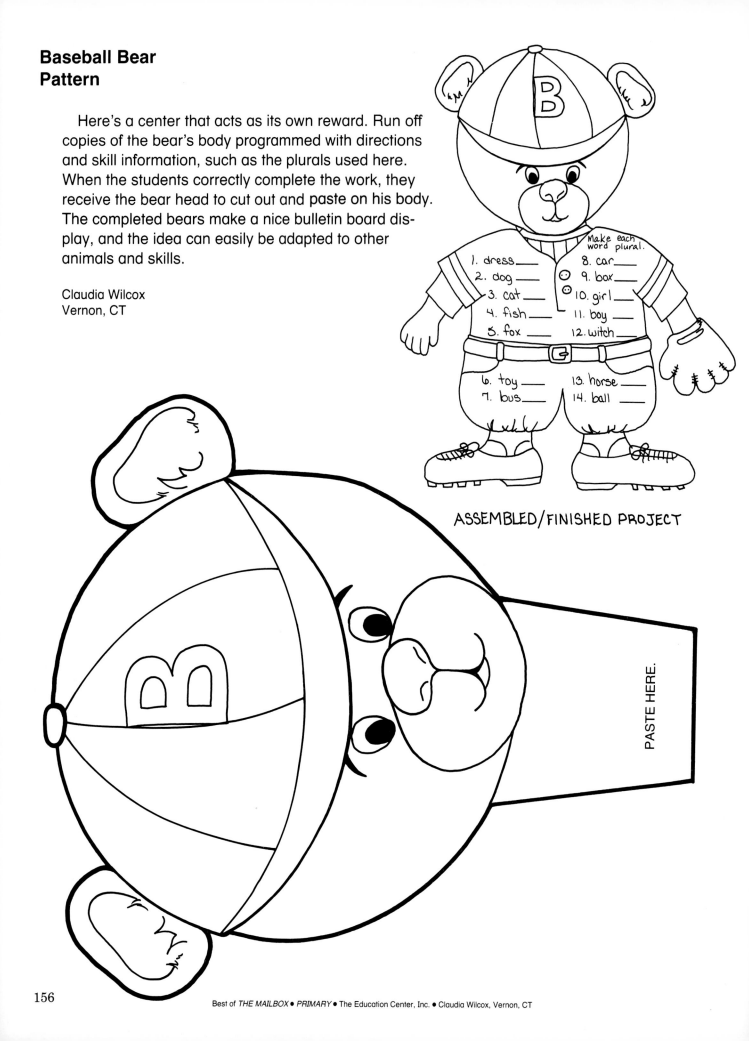

Make each word plural.

1. dress____   8. car____
2. dog____   9. box____
3. cat____   10. girl____
4. fish____   11. boy____
5. fox____   12. witch____
6. toy____   13. horse____
7. bus____   14. ball____

ASSEMBLED/FINISHED PROJECT

PASTE HERE.

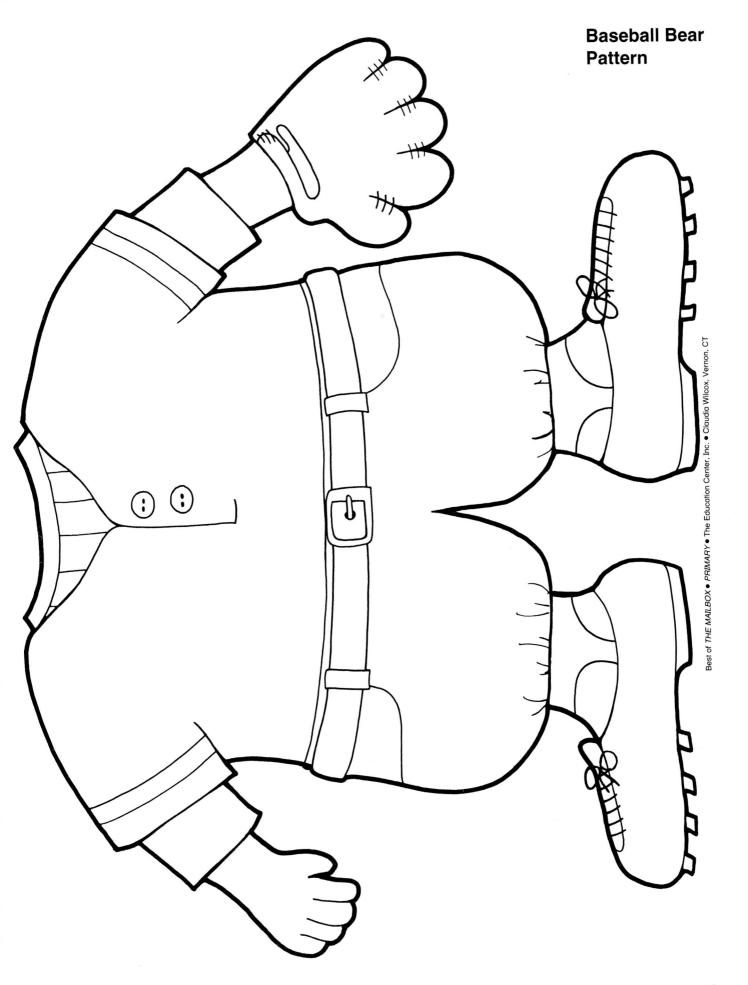

Best of *THE MAILBOX* • *PRIMARY* • The Education Center, Inc. • Claudia Wilcox, Vernon, CT

Paper Cup Puppet Pattern

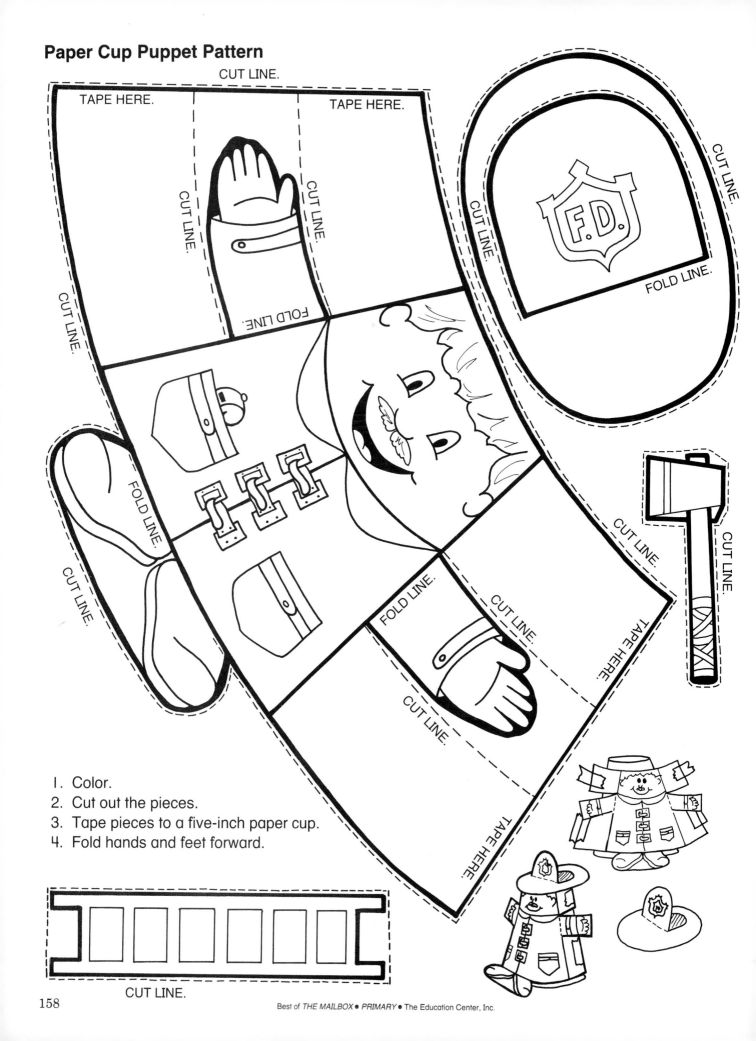

CUT LINE.

TAPE HERE.

TAPE HERE.

CUT LINE.

CUT LINE.

CUT LINE.

FOLD LINE.

F.D.

FOLD LINE.

CUT LINE.

CUT LINE.

FOLD LINE.

FOLD LINE.

CUT LINE.

CUT LINE.

TAPE HERE.

CUT LINE.

CUT LINE.

TAPE HERE.

1. Color.
2. Cut out the pieces.
3. Tape pieces to a five-inch paper cup.
4. Fold hands and feet forward.

CUT LINE.

Buford

Excuse me!

Please.

Thank you!

Note To Teacher: Make a milk carton supply holder with Buford the Mouse! While Buford politely holds crayons, flash cards, or game pieces, he'll remind students to always use their best manners.

Reversible Duck/Rabbit Pattern

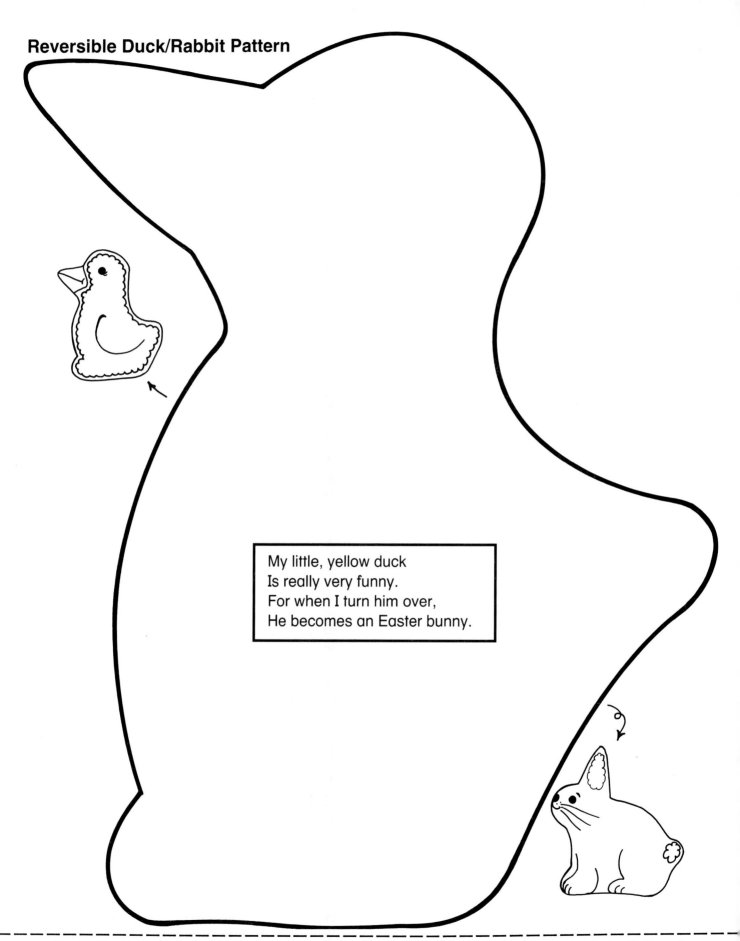

My little, yellow duck
Is really very funny.
For when I turn him over,
He becomes an Easter bunny.

Note To Teacher: Duplicate on white construction paper. On one side of pattern, student glues cotton as shown and colors it with a yellow marker. He colors an orange beak and adds a black, cut-out eye and details with a black marker. On the other side, he adds a white, cotton rabbit tail. He glues cotton in the ear and colors it pink, then draws nose, eye, mouth, whiskers, and feet.

Name _____

Elephant Blends

Write a blend from the blend bank that will make a word.

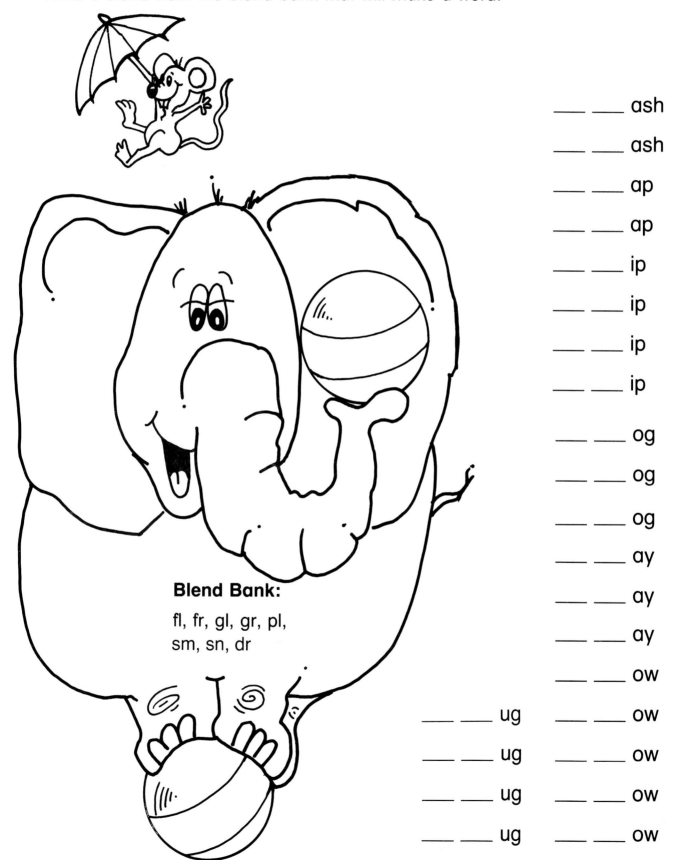

Blend Bank:

fl, fr, gl, gr, pl,
sm, sn, dr

___ ___ ash

___ ___ ash

___ ___ ap

___ ___ ap

___ ___ ip

___ ___ ip

___ ___ ip

___ ___ ip

___ ___ og

___ ___ og

___ ___ og

___ ___ ay

___ ___ ay

___ ___ ay

___ ___ ow

___ ___ ug   ___ ___ ow

___ ___ ug   ___ ___ ow

___ ___ ug   ___ ___ ow

___ ___ ug   ___ ___ ow

Vowel Owl

Fill in the blank with the correct diphthong **ow** or **ou**.

___ l	h ___ se
cl ___ n	c ___
sc ___ t	cl ___ d
___ t	sh ___ t
p ___ der	br ___ n
m ___ ntain	ab ___ t
cr ___ d	bl ___ se
fl ___ er	n ___
t ___ el	m ___ se

Best of THE MAILBOX • PRIMARY • The Education Center, Inc. • Terri Sheldon, Honolulu, HI   Answer keys on pages 190 and 191.

Gee! Look At The Cheese!

1. Color **Ginger** and the **soft G** sound cheeses orange. Color **Gary** and the **hard G** sound cheeses yellow.

2. Cut out the mice and cheeses.

3. Fold a piece of construction paper in half. Paste Ginger on one half and Gary on the other. Paste the cheeses under the correct mouse.

Ginger

Gary

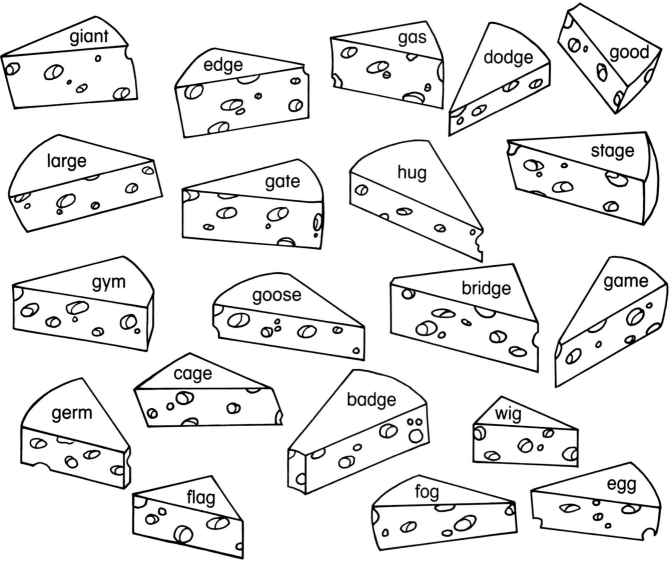

giant

edge

gas

dodge

good

large

gate

hug

stage

gym

goose

bridge

game

cage

germ

badge

wig

flag

fog

egg

The "Bear" Facts

1. Subtract each of these numbers—896, 784, 518—from 2,164.

2. Add all of these numbers... 512, 691, 827, 777, and subtract $(5 \times 9)-6$ from the total.

3. Divide these numbers by 9... 810, 630, 540, 360, 270, 720.

4. Add each of these numbers to ninety-four...
   twenty-seven
   nineteen
   forty-six
   thirty-eight

5. Add $\frac{1}{4}$ to each of these numbers... $5\frac{1}{2}$, $6\frac{3}{4}$, $9\frac{5}{8}$.

6. Add 395 to each of these numbers... 437, 685, 29.

7. Write down all even numbers from 900 to 930. Do the same for odd numbers.

8. Add 5 to each of these numbers... IX, V, VII, XIV, XXIV.

Answer keys on pages 190 and 191.

How To Make A Jack-o'-Lantern

Write these sentences in the correct order below.

I need a broomstick! Save your straw from lunch. Cut on the dotted lines; then insert your straw.

Scoop out the pulp and seeds.
Place a candle inside your pumpkin.
Carve your pumpkin's face.
Buy a large pumpkin.
Light the candle.
Draw a face on your pumpkin.
Watch your jack-o'-lantern glow!
Cut a top on the pumpkin.

1.	
2.	
3.	
4.	
5.	
6.	
7.	
8.	

Answer keys on pages 190 and 191.

The Best of THE MAILBOX • PRIMARY • The Education Center, Inc. • Katie Baily, Bristol, CT

There Was An Old Witch

There was an old witch, believe it if you can,

She tapped on the windows and she ran, ran, ran.

She ran helter-skelter with her toes in the air,

Cornstalks flying from the old witch's hair!

"Swish," goes the broomstick, "Me-ow," goes the cat,

"Plop," goes the hoptoad sitting on her hat.

"Whee," chuckled I, "What fun! What fun!"

Halloween night when the witches run.

(Author unknown)

1. Draw a blue line under all compound words.
2. Put a small red x above two words that rhyme with bat.
3. Draw two lines with your pencil under each word that has the short sound of *i* as in little.
4. Put a big orange x on a word that means almost the same as laughed.
5. Draw a red ring around a word that is the opposite of day.
6. Put two orange lines under a word with a hyphen that tells how the witch ran.
7. Draw a picture of the poem on the back of this paper.

Best of THE MAILBOX ● *PRIMARY* ● The Education Center, Inc. ● Trudy McGuire, Gladstone, OK   Answer keys on pages 190 and 191.

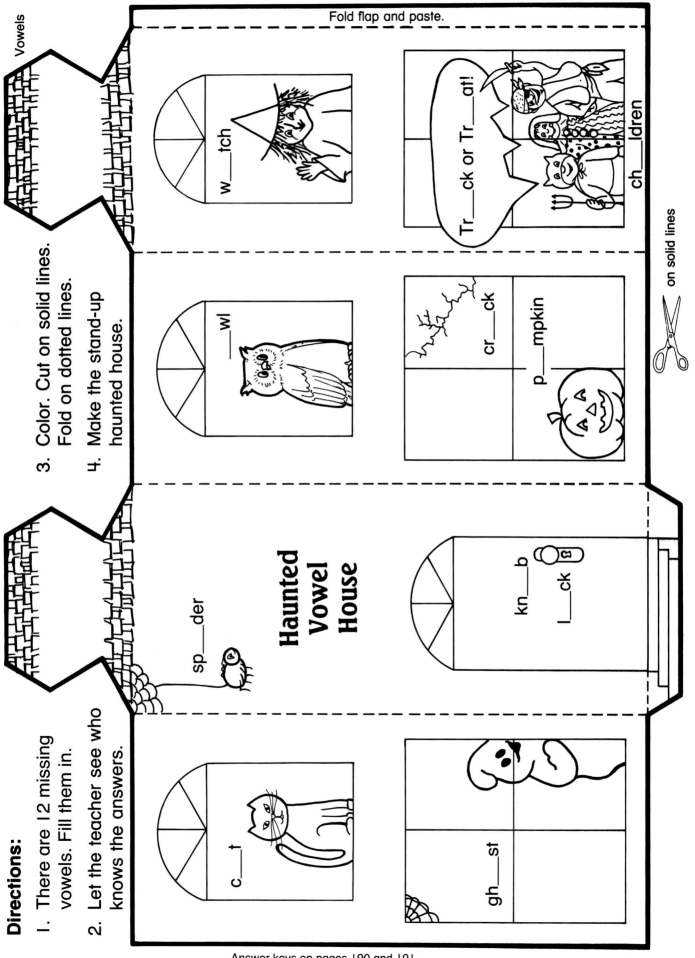

Vowels

Fold flap and paste.

w__tch

Tr__ck or Tr__at!

ch__ldren

on solid lines

3. Color. Cut on solid lines. Fold on dotted lines.

4. Make the stand-up haunted house.

__wl

cr__ck

p__mpkin

Directions:

1. There are 12 missing vowels. Fill them in.

2. Let the teacher see who knows the answers.

Haunted Vowel House

sp__der

kn__b

l__ck

c__t

gh__st

Best of THE MAILBOX • PRIMARY • The Education Center, Inc. • Mary Dinneen, Bristol, CT

Dreidel Daze

The dreidel is a favorite toy of Jewish children. It is used for a special game during Hanukkah. The dreidel is a four-sided top with a Hebrew letter written on each side.

To play, each child puts the same number of candies, nuts, or other treats into a pile. The children take turns spinning the dreidel. When the dreidel falls, the letter showing on the top tells the spinner what he can do:

nun	נ	take **nothing** from the pile
gimmel	ג	take **all** of the treats
heh	ה	take **half** of the treats
shin	ש	**put** a number of "goodies" into the pile

1. A _____ is a four-sided top used during Hanukkah.

2. The toy is used in a game by _____ children.

3. A _____ letter is written on each side of the top.

4. Players put a number of nuts, candies, or _____ into a pile.

5. If the player spins the letter *gimmel*, he takes _____ from the pile.

6. If *nun* is showing, the player takes _____ from the pile.

7. The spinner takes half of the goodies if _____ shows on the top.

8. _____ means the player must add to the pile in the center.

Here's how to make your own dreidel toy.
1. Cut a 1½-inch square from an index card.
2. Draw lines from corner to corner.
3. Punch a hole in the center of the card where the lines cross.
4. Trace or cut out the Hebrew letters above. Paste them on the card.
5. Put a round, wooden toothpick in the center hole.
6. Play the dreidel game with your family or friends.

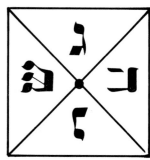

Partridge In A Pear Tree

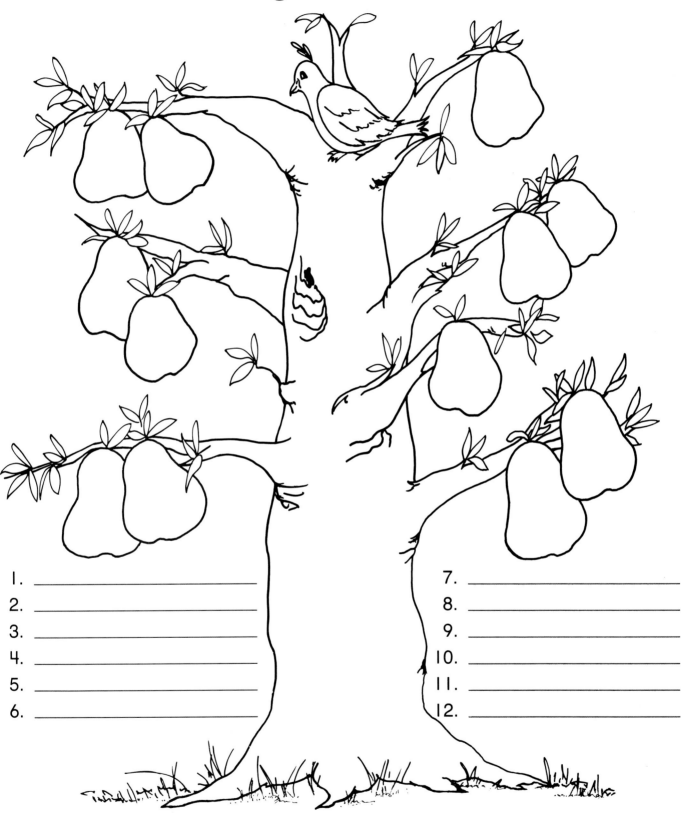

1. _____
2. _____
3. _____
4. _____
5. _____
6. _____

7. _____
8. _____
9. _____
10. _____
11. _____
12. _____

Note To Teacher: Use this open worksheet for any sequencing skill: ABC order, number or story sequence. Write the words, numbers, or letters in the pears before duplicating.

Name _____

Santa's List

Note To Teacher: Write your students' names in the squares for a word search. Add names to Santa's List for answer bank.

Trim The Tree

Add ornaments to the tree by drawing a circle around each of the long-vowel words.

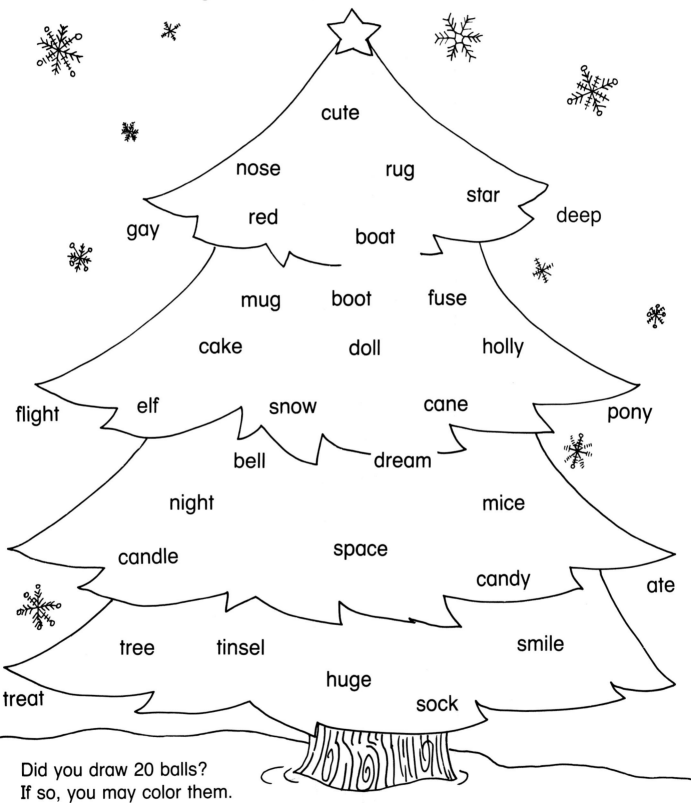

cute

nose   rug

star

red   deep

gay   boat

mug   boot   fuse

cake   doll   holly

flight   elf   snow   cane   pony

bell   dream

night   mice

space

candle

candy   ate

tree   tinsel   smile

treat   huge   sock

Did you draw 20 balls?
If so, you may color them.

Answer keys on pages 190 and 191.

Snowman Delight

Fill in
the blanks.

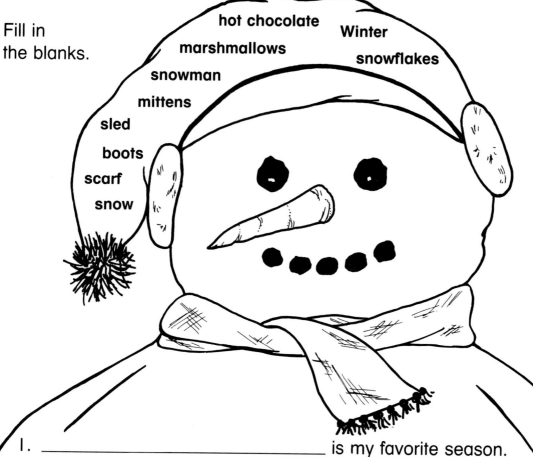

hot chocolate
Winter
marshmallows
snowflakes
snowman
mittens
sled
boots
scarf
snow

1. _____ is my favorite season.

2. Everyone wears _____ to keep their feet dry.

3. The sisters have red _____ to wear on their hands.

4. Your neck will stay warm if you wear a _____.

5. Rob and Roy like to play with their _____ in the snow.

6. Buffy chases _____ as they fall.

7. The boys always build a _____.

8. We get cold when we play in the _____.

9. Don't you like to drink _____
   after playing outside?

10. Jenny likes _____
    in her hot chocolate.

Answer keys on pages 190 and 191.

Mr. Lincoln's Hat

Make Abe's hat "grow."

1. Paste Mr. Lincoln on 12" × 18" construction paper the long way.
2. Work problems on scrap paper.
3. Fill in answers and cut sections apart.
4. On Abe's hat, paste sections together in order from low to high numbers.

93 – 5 =
72 – 43 =
50 – 25 =
61 – 9 =
65 – 27 =
94 – 58 =
81 – 34 =
76 – 18 =
93 – 19 =
92 – 21 =

Assembled project

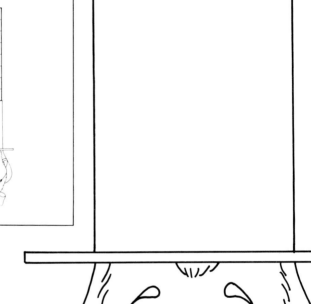

Answer keys on pages 190 and 191.

Valentine Mail

Write the addresses correctly on lined paper.

29 stafford avenue
06001
dr thomas hunter
boston massachusetts

mrs lisa brooks
hartford connecticut
06342
534 main street

fido puppy
01234
puppytown illinois
1 doghouse lane

BE MINE!

Fido

Bonus Box: Make a valentine to put in one of these mailboxes.

Answer keys on pages 190 and 191.

Best of THE MAILBOX ● PRIMARY ● The Education Center, Inc. ● Kathleen Baily, Avon, CT

Valentine's Day Mail

is not	it is
did not	we will
can not	I would
we are	are not
will not	do not
I will	I have

Write the words on the envelopes.

I'll	won't	isn't
1 — I will	2	3

it's	don't	can't
4	5	6

I'd	we're	didn't
7	8	9

we'll	aren't	I've
10	11	12

Meg's Eggs

Rhymes with **day**, color it **red**.
Rhymes with **do**, color it **yellow**.
Rhymes with **my**, color it **blue**.
Rhymes with **hit**, color it **orange**.
Rhymes with **cat**, color it **green**.

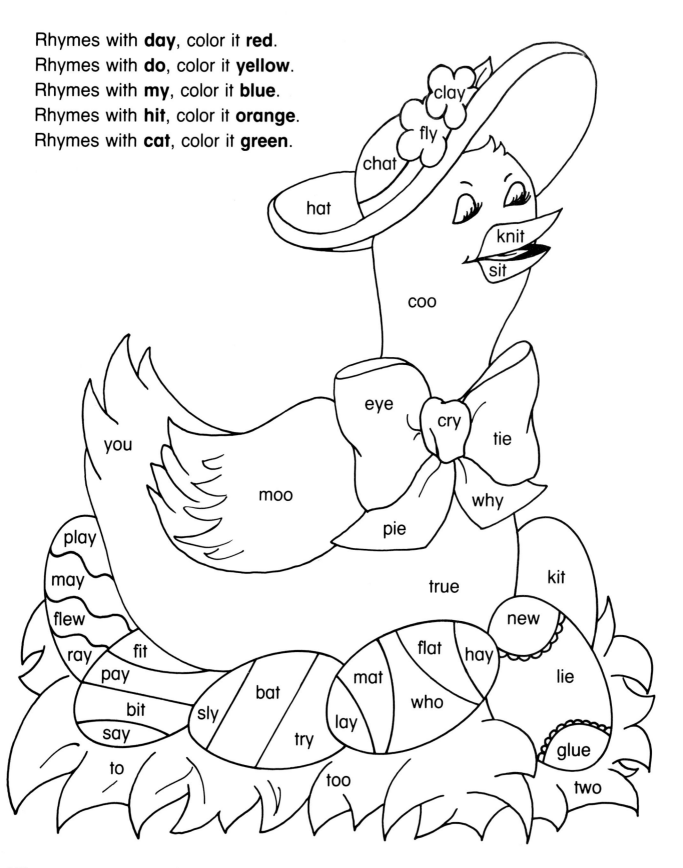

Funny Bunny Code

Use the code on the eggs to make these short *e* words.

1. $\underset{1}{e}$ $\underset{6}{}$ $\underset{6}{}$

2. $\underset{2}{}$ $\underset{1}{}$ $\underset{3}{}$

3. $\underset{5}{}$ $\underset{1}{}$ $\underset{2}{}$

4. $\underset{10}{}$ $\underset{7}{}$ $\underset{1}{}$ $\underset{4}{}$

5. $\underset{3}{}$ $\underset{1}{}$ $\underset{2}{}$ $\underset{3}{}$

6. $\underset{11}{}$ $\underset{1}{}$ $\underset{7}{}$ $\underset{7}{}$

7. $\underset{9}{}$ $\underset{1}{}$ $\underset{4}{}$

8. $\underset{2}{}$ $\underset{1}{}$ $\underset{10}{}$ $\underset{3}{}$

9. $\underset{11}{}$ $\underset{1}{}$ $\underset{12}{}$

10. $\underset{8}{}$ $\underset{1}{}$ $\underset{2}{}$

Now color the eggs.

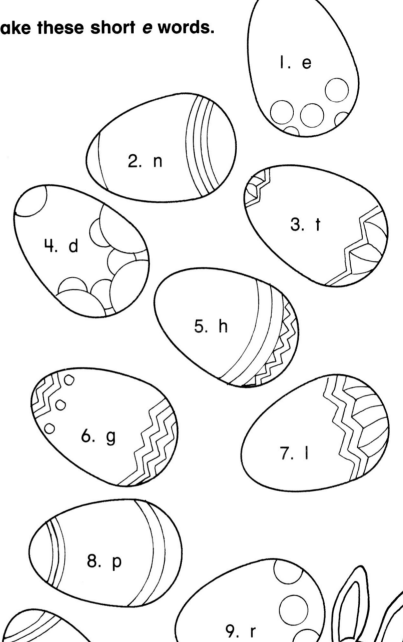

1. e
2. n
3. t
4. d
5. h
6. g
7. l
8. p
9. r
10. s
11. w
12. b

Step-by-Step Rabbit

1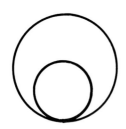

2

3

4

5

6

7

Draw a bunny in this box step-by-step.